In My Wildest Dreams…And More

By

Ruth Marston Carwile

authorHOUSE®

Published by AuthorHouse 05/21/2015

ISBN: 978-1-4184-9241-0 (sc)

Print information available on the last page.

This book is printed on acid-free paper.

Table of Contents

In My Wildest Dreams

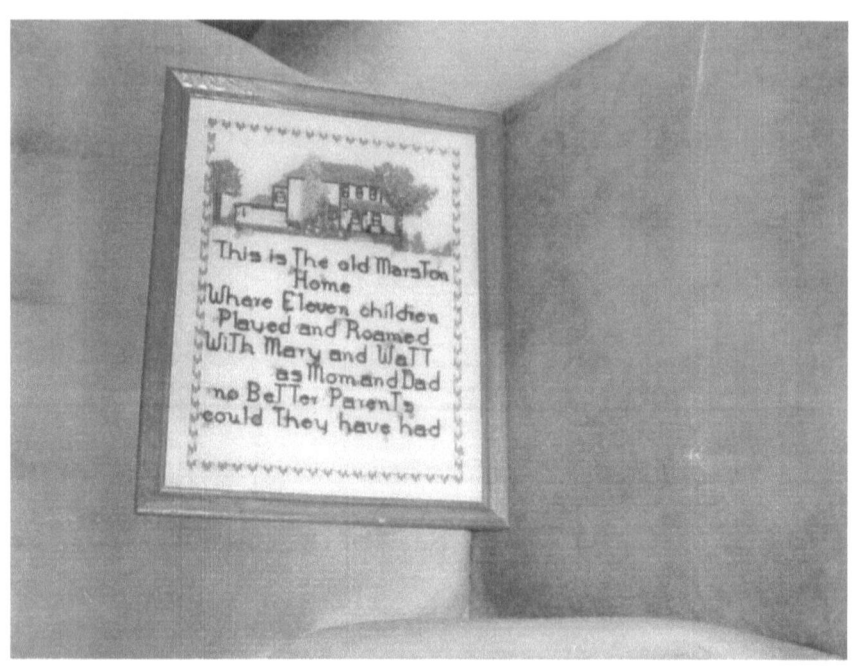

Made by Dorothy Trent, age 91

"The Old Marston Home"

Dedication

This book is dedicated to my nephew, Marvin Grey Arrington, the first to proofread, and with this note of encouragement and inspiration to edit it. Marvin passed away June 30, 2000 leaving a legacy of his own: of developed technology in his field and friends and fond memories for all whose lives he touched.

(1947-2000)

Preface

Today, November, 1999, as I, Ruth Marston Carwile, stand on the brink of another year, another century and yes, another millennium and also my eightieth birthday, I will try to portray to you, my readers, some of the changes which I have witnessed over the span of those years:

I, like every young person, hoped and dreamed of a prosperous fulfilling life, but in my wildest dreams and youthful imagery could never have foreseen the dramatic changes in scientific and medical technology, social and economic development and in every phase of life, as I have seen transpire over the past 50 years. I once had a Sunday School teacher who, in her mind, would explain in metaphor, how all inventions, discoveries, etc. are made possible for us. She said they are as apples already on a tree which God lowers, within reach of man, giving him the ability to attain them, and the natural gifts and talents to develop them, in His own Providential time and way.

If that be true, never before in history has God been so busy "lowering apples" nor has He given mankind so much knowledge, skill and ability to develop them as in the past 50 years. Even today, when we are so blessed as never before with modern conveniences, technology, etc., each new day brings newness on the horizon, with much of the old becoming obsolete. After so many changes, the carnal mind tells me that there cannot be many more "apples" left on the tree to be developed, but the Spiritual instincts ring out loud and clear - "My Father worketh still and so do I" John 5:17!! Please follow me now as I reflect on these ever changing times.

Chapter 1

Perhaps no place on earth is more vividly or rightly named than "Rolling Hill, Virginia," the beautiful, remote countryside of Charlotte County where I was born. Remote? Did we know it? No, but in retrospect as my story unfolds - well, the decision will be yours.

My maternal grandparents, Luther and Mary Casper Rhodenhizer (Cassie) Elder were life-long residents of this predominantly tobacco farming section of western Charlotte County with ownership of a several hundred acre farm inherited by my granddaddy. Its rich heritage and ownership going back several generations.

My grandfather served as magistrate for Charlotte County, holding trials in his home with us enjoying the proceedings from behind the doors. I remember as a child, going back several generations of trials, recorded in the "law" books in granddaddy's desk (later destroyed by fire). My grandmother Cassie's father, William Rhodenhizer, came from a family of iron masters and had migrated from Callands, near Danville, Virginia to Rolling Hill and established a foundry there, a much needed industry of the times. In his foundry he made plow points for horse drawn plows, horseshoes, grubbing hoes, axes, wash pots and many other modern conveniences of the day.

Granny and Granddaddy
Elder

Granny Elder's sister, Carrie
Rhodenhizer

Granny told us many stories of her youth, how her mother died early in life, leaving her to care for her younger brothers, Henry, who later owned and operated a foundry in Keysville, Virginia; Walker, Jeff, Chap and John, also sisters Eula, Pattie, Carrie and another sister who died as an infant from a fire in the family fireplace. Then as granny said, along came a handsome, stately young man from a few miles up the road, Luther Elder, bringing her a pound of Brazil nuts for a Christmas gift. I can still hear her chuckle as she related that story to us. Anyway, it had its lasting rewards: a beautiful marriage, which spanned over six decades, culminating into a family of five daughters, Mary, Leona, Emma, Eula, Florine, Janie and Norma Lee, and four boys, Elbert, Henry, Corbin and Len, also living to enjoy their many grandchildren and great-grandchildren.

When my mother, Mary, the eldest of granddaddy's and granny's daughters, was 15, my dad, Watson Lewellyn Marston (Watt), the son of Robert and Mary Palmer Elder Marston, from the Hat Creek community of adjoining

Campbell County, some 18 or 20 miles away, came by horse and buggy all the way to Rolling Hill to meet Mary through a mutual friend, Bernard Elder. Watt, already 25 and not willing to continue driving his horse and buggy that distance over dirt and muddy roads in all kinds of weather, soon proposed to Mary. She being only 15 and legally underage for marriage in Virginia, they decided to "run away" to be married, as it was called in that day. They boarded a Norfolk and Western train in Brookneal, Virginia, for Roxboro, North Carolina, obtaining license and marrying the same day. They were accompanied by Bernard Elder, and dad's brother, Elva Marston, as necessary witnesses.

Dad often laughed as he told us the story of how granddaddy Elder greeted them upon their return home. Dad said granddaddy didn't even speak to them and as daddy phrased it, "he just walked around with his lip poked out." Daddy in his usual wit said to him, "If you don't take that lip in you will step on it." That broke the ice, helping to create a bond of life-long friendship, always helping each other, with daddy turning to granddaddy for advice and fatherly wisdom in many areas of his life.

Daddy and mama then moved to the tobacco farm at Hat Creek, which he jointly owned with his sister and brother-in-law, Cornelia and Dick Elder. Daddy had already built a two or three room house which is still standing today after weathering some 85 years, its boards still sound because as daddy said, he "kiln" dried the timbers before building it. He was already using his exact and thorough, and sometimes, maybe, the hardest way of accomplishing a task - and I thought in growing up, it was a characteristic he had just acquired to practice on us!! His philosophy - "Do it well or not at all."

The first of their, eventually eleven children, Pauline (Polly) was born there at Hat Creek, two years later Evelyn was born there, also. After several years at Hat Creek, daddy sold his portion of the farm to Uncle Dick and purchased a farm at Rolling Hill from a black man by the name of Billy King. I wish I knew more about him, only as a child I remember our farm was referred to as the "Billy King farm." It was located a few miles across Bear Creek from Mama's birthplace. She was back home at last. The story goes, that Billy King was burned out by some jealous people of his own race— stable, horses and all. He must have been very prosperous to have owned such a fine, fertile farm.

Daddy and mama, Polly and Evelyn moved into a house consisting of a log room, a shed room on two sides and a front porch in between. There I, Ruth, was born in that log room, January 25, 1920. They say it was raining, heavily sleeting, so rough that Dr. Luken could not get there from Pamplin. A neighbor midwife, Celia Thornton delivered me. Dr. Luken came the next day, by horseback. I have only faint memories of my two or three years in that house. Only one stands out, daddy was sitting on the front porch reading the Bible and a rabid or as they were called, mad dog, came around the house and suddenly attacked daddy and on impulse, while kicking the dog, he threw the Bible at it. The torn Bible was always a reminder of its different blessings in varied times of need.

By this time, about age three, I have memories of seeing a new house being built just up the hill from our cabin. Another sister, Christine, was born there also. Our new white frame house was large enough, with seven rooms and two halls, to accommodate the growing family eventually to be born there; Rachel and Charlotte (by this time, six girls) but they didn't give up; finally a boy, Watson Lee (later killed at age 12) then Benny, Ryland and twin boys, Renneth and Kenneth.

Watt and Mary Marston's Family
Front row: Benny, Watt, Renneth, Mary, Kenneth, and Ryland
Back row: Polly, Evelyn, Ruth, Christine, Rachel, and Charlotte

Now that you know something about my family I shall tell you more about the customs of the times.

We grew up around a wood burning fireplace, which was in mama's and daddy's bedroom, and I have so many childhood memories of family togetherness on winter nights and snowy days playing card games like Rook and Old Maid (but no card games on the Sabbath.) Daddy and I were strong opponents in checker games. Our oldest sister, Polly, would sometimes read to the family, one book in particular, John Bunyan's "Pilgrims Progress" which I still remember. We would pop popcorn in a wire popcorn popper over the fire, eat apples which had been garnered from the orchard (every farm had an orchard; apples, peaches, pears, cherries, etc.) and stored in barrels for winter. The Stayman Winesap apple was the best for long keeping and for cooking and eating. We would make popcorn balls and how good was the snow cream!

All Elder children of Cassie and Luther to right) Norma Adams, Len Elder, Mary Marston, Elbert Elder, Eula Guthrie, Henry Elder, Florine Harper, Emma McCollough, Corbin Elder, and Leona Marston

Granny and Granddaddy Elder's 50th Wedding Anniversary Corbin, Leona (Lee Lee), Norma Lee, Henry, Granny, Mary, Granddaddy, Emma, Eula, Elbert, Florine and Len

Ruth Marston Carwile

Florine Harper, Leona Marston, Eula Guthrie, Norma Adams,
Henry Elder

Uncle Mack Marston

Granddaddy Luther Elder
and Grandma Cassie Elder
(*Fiftieth Anniversary*)

Uncle Mack's wife, Leonia
(Lee Lee)
90th Birthday

Kenneth and Renneth Marston

Bedtime meant going to cold upstairs bedrooms, no heat, but at times with a warm flat iron at our feet.

The snows were deeper and I believe more frequent back in those days, bringing the family closer together in love and affection. I still love the poem "Snowbound" by John Greenleaf Whittier which tells in bright imagery of a farm cut off by a snowfall as though he could have been describing ours. I still experience that feeling of childhood excitement when we have a beautiful snowfall, even though I now live alone.

About the time daddy and mama moved back to Rolling Hill, daddy's brother, Mack, and Mama's sister, Leona, whom we affectionately call Lee Lee, were married and bought a farm-adjoining daddy's with only a creek separating the two families. The blood kinship, making us double first cousins to Helen, Thomas, Dean, Nancy and Merle, but one big family in relationship, keeping a well trodden path between our homes. Recently I visited with Lee Lee who is still in sound mind and body at age 96, and she told me of experiences from their early years of marriage. She said the first year she and Uncle Mack were married, they were living in an old cabin on the farm. One night her brother, Elbert, was visiting them from up the road when they heard a noise coming from the woods, they were all scared to death, thinking it was a wild cat. Elbert needed to go home so she and Uncle Mack walked with him part of the way with Uncle Mack carrying a wagon standard for their protection. When they got up to the highway, the noise broke out again. Elbert started running, stopping only when he got home and Uncle Mack took off running back to their home, carrying the wagon standard with him, leaving her there all alone. She said when they got in the house they propped furniture against the door, got in bed and covered their heads, not stirring all night. The next morning, they ventured out on the front porch and lo and behold the bobcat turned out to be a mother dog and her starving pups. She said the mother dog later went away, leaving her puppies there for them to care for. I'm sure the mother dog knew what mature and responsible hands she was leaving her pups in. Lee Lee was so cute as she told about Uncle Mack running back to the house carrying the wagon standard with him. She said, "and Mack never wanted to hear about it again, but Mr. Elijah Ramsey, a neighbor, never let him forget it." Uncle Mack, now deceased, lived to be 97 years of age.

She also told me during that visit, about Granny Elder's father, William Rhodenhizer, who was a soldier in the Civil War. The day that Lee surrendered, her grandfather, William, walked from Appomattox, then followed the path, which we always used across from our house and on by her house just down the road to his home and foundry at Rolling Hill. From now on this will enhance my memory walk over the hills and across the peaceful stream of flowing water which is often before me even in my dreams. How hallowed that walk must have been for William Rhodenhizer as he returned home from a war of bloodshed and cannonfire. We owe so much to those who have walked before. History says it was on a Sunday, April 9, 1865, when Robert E. Lee surrendered to a strong, cigar chewing, Grant. It also tells us that each Confederate soldier was released on parole with one full day's rations and was allowed to keep his horse. William Rhodenhizer could have been a foot soldier or perhaps his horse was shot from under him.

Chapter 2

Transportation and Communication

    From our house to my grandparents home, to Lee Lee's and Uncle Macks, to Mr. and Mrs. Ed Wilbun's farm, adjoining on another side to Mr and Mrs. McFee's also, there were walking paths and the welcome mats were always out. Mama and daddy along with all of us children, would go often after supper and "sit 'til bedtime" with daddy carrying the oil lantern as we paraded behind mama and him to visit the neighbors. I can still see our shadows across the dark fields and hear the peaceful sound of crickets as we walked by, then they would pay our visit back. There was always plenty of time; no one seemed to be in a hurry. Money was nobody's priority. Another means of transportation was the horse and buggy and in our case, the mules and surrey for the extended trips, like visiting relatives at Hat Creek, some 15 miles away. Maybe the people of our area were not as rushed but dad's mules, Dinah and Adah were! They were always raring to go and often "running away!" When we were children playing in the yard we would hear daddy yell out - that meant get in the house - Dinah and Adah were on the rampage and running away. We had a two seated surrey (a Cadillac in its day) snap on curtains with celluloid windows with oil lamps on each side. Daddy took a lot of pride in Dinah and Adah, currying, combing and brushing them and I can remember how proud he would look when someone would say, "Watt, you have a fine looking team." Back then, all country roads were unpaved, sometimes muddy with deep wagon ruts. Dinah and Adah seemed to know they were carrying precious cargo most of the time with mama, daddy and a surrey full of children and behaved as such....that is, until we happened to meet an automobile on the road. Daddy would pull over to the side of the road and stop, holding the reins with all his might until the "big monster" passed on!!

Only a few people around there owned a car at that time. Granddaddy Elder bought a Model T Ford and how scared I was going over deep, muddy ruts and his driving all over the road. Rubber tires were so inferior and there would be a flat tire every few miles, but that was just added recreation for us children on the way.

One evening we were late leaving our grandparent's home at Hat Creek; on the way darkness overtook us. The modern lamps were there on the surrey, but we had no matches, so we stopped at a house (now on highway 600, I believe a Roach family lived there, formerly the Hamlet farm and then Evans) and Polly, our oldest sister, always taking the initiative, went in and borrowed a match, then there was light!! and daddy didn't even have to dim them.

The surrey was our means of transportation until daddy bought a new 1928, green touring Chevrolet car which also had curtains to be snapped on and off, according to the weather. Of course, daddy had to learn to drive the new car so Manly Holt, a salesman for Lawson Motor Company, in Brookneal carried mama and daddy driving, with daddy at the wheel.

Going over the wooded road through the farm up to Rolling Hill Road, daddy's driving lessons were over. Now daddy knew how to drive, he didn't even have to have a driving permit. Then Manly had mama get under the wheel to drive back; not so successful for mama, she got a severe migraine headache and never attempted to drive again. (I doubt if Mr. Holt had life insurance.) Daddy said he was undecided about buying the car at first when mama said to him, "If I were to die, you would buy one." that did it so he said, "Manly, I'll take the car." This was in 1928, the economy was good - daddy's tobacco prices were affording a good living for the ever-growing family. Mama and Byrd Bagby, the black woman living on the farm with her husband, Jerry and their children, would make off orders to Sears Roebuck, Chicago Mail Order and other mail order companies for our shoes, winter coats, etc. Mama would always let us select our own. She even ordered a linoleum runner for the hallway in our home!!! Blue and white checks - the first floor covering we ever had or had seen. How happy we were, it was so shiny and pretty. Two porches were added to the house, even money in the bank.

1915 Model T

1925 Ford Model T

1926 Ford Model TT

1929 Model A

1930 Ford

"Photos graciously provided by Harvey Elder Dealership, VA."

Ford 1932   1940 Ford

1950 Ford Custom

1952 Ford   1956 T-Bird

"Photos graciously provided by Harvey Elder Dealership, VA."

57 FORD T-BIRD

1966 Ford Mustang

TOREADOR RED 2001
CLEARCOAT METALLIC

"Photos graciously provided by Harvey Elder Dealership, VA."

THE ROARING 20' S

During the 1920's, World War 1 was over, Ford cars were available and everyone was enjoying a sense of security and freedom, especially were the "flappers" with an unrestricted use of cosmetics, short skirts and bobbed hair. As a child, how I did admire Mama's teenage sisters, Florine and Eula during those roaring 20's. They had plenty of make up, the rouge, Heather, I remember the name of it in a paper box, which I would use, if I had a chance. They had a hair curling iron which they would heat inside the lamp chimney and high heel shoes, which I enjoyed tipping around in. Eula and Florine are now deceased, but I talked with Ollie Harper

Sublett now 94 years of age, and in sound mind, bringing me up to date as she hilariously reminisced. Ollie, a cousin of Florine and Eula, would come up from Phenix, Virginia, for extended visits with them, bringing even more make-up for my enjoyment. She said they wore short dresses which showed their black bloomers and later, how thrilled they were when they came out with real pretty brown colored bloomers. These had ruffles on the legs and they would wear colored garters at the top of the ruffles. In Ollie's witty way she said they would show the garters as much as they dared to. She also said, if you didn't have a spit curl you didn't have anything! They glued a curl right in the middle of the forehead with spit or with soap, she said. Another fad was to roll silk stockings just below the short hemline, wearing open goloshes, a long string of beads reaching almost to the dress hemline, also a close fitting "Cloche" hat completed the outfit. Ollie said she wore a navy blue cloche hat when she and Warren were married. Ollie also said, her boyfriend had a one seated Model T Ford with only one door and that was on the passenger's side. The boyfriend would help Eula and her in the car, go around to the front of the car, crank it hurriedly, crawl over Eula and her to the steering wheel. She said Henry, Corbin and Len, Eula's younger brothers, would be around the corner of the house watching and laughing their hearts out. She said how embarrassed she and Eula were! I remember all Model T Fords were cranked by hand in front of the car. When it finally fired, the driver would hurriedly run around the car, jump in to adjust the mechanisms on the steering wheel, to keep it running. At times, the crank would "kick", so to speak. Many arms were broken in this way, including Henry's. If all couldn't ride in the car, they would stand on the running board on both sides. That, too, caused many falling accidents. Once Eula fell on a rock, causing a mild concussion, I now believe, every driver enjoyed blowing the horn of the Model T Ford, a very unforgettable and unique sound. Before rounding a curve every driver would bear down on the horn, seemingly giving him a feeling of power and self importance. There were no women drivers in our area at that time.

Music played an important role in the 20's. Ollie said they would gather around her playing the old pump organ at Granny's and the fun they would have singing the old favorites, "Girl of my Dreams"; "Sweet Bunch of Daisies"; "Yes we Have No Bananas". I also remember them singing "Roll 'em, Roll 'em, Roll 'em Down and show your Pretty knees", and they did!! Emma would also play the old pump organ and all singing with Claude's deep voice coming in on "Dwelling in Beulah Land, "When the Roll Is Called Up Yonder" and many others.

Everything seemed to be prosperous and going well when on October 29, 1929, as dad came home from the tobacco market and stopped by the bank in Brookneal, the doors were closed. The bank was "broke" as was the term used then and it truly was! All because the stock market in New York went broke. I didn't understand any of it then (as far as I knew stock consisted of animals on the farm) only how it hurt me to see my mother and dad suffer for loss of their savings - a lot for those days - outstanding checks and no way to buy necessities for their children. The bottom also dropped out of the tobacco market - dad spread the tobacco on the orchard and I remember they carried us to a Halloween program at Red House School that night, which we were to participate in. As always, putting family first. I remember mama telling our teacher, Miss Annie Lee Sprinkle that night about the bank closing and about her having only 50-cents left and outstanding checks to be paid. How could they have attended a Halloween party and program that night? Now I see they were already exerting the stamina and resiliency, which they had and would need for almost a decade of depression to come. "When the going gets tough, the tough gets going!" The bank kept hopes up by promises to pay dividends but very little was ever paid, maybe a 5% payment once or twice. Hoover was president then of our country and every parent who had to provide for the family, and even the children, never outlived the memories of "Hoover's times" as they have been called. The sharp contrast in every way would be unbelievable to those who are living in today's society. It had been said that Hoover's campaign slogan was the promise of a "car in every garage and a chicken in every pot." Well, he was correct about the car - the beautiful green '28 car was parked in the garage and there it stayed for years to come. There was no money for license, gas, etc. Dad put blocks under the wheels to protect the tires. The depression was in full force, but life had to go on, neighbor helping neighbor. When daddy bought the farm, there was very little cleared land on which to grow crops. Neighbors would get together and have what they called "cutting matches," cutting down trees from land to be cleared, also for firewood, curing tobacco in barns and also for the cooking stove which was used both summer and winter. But those cutting matches were not all work. Neighbors enjoyed getting together and especially at lunchtime. In those days there were no power saws. Each man had ground his ax razor sharp. And that I do know. I had to turn the grindstone for daddy, forever it seemed. And I believe the coldest days of the year. The crosscut saw was pulled by two men – one on each end. After the trees were cleared off, the new ground had to be cultivated with a hoe-like plow called a colter, pulled by a mule to get up roots. We children had our jobs, too, picking up and piling roots to be burned. After many times of picking up and piling roots the land was ready for planting tobacco, the only money crop. The tobacco plants were transplanted from a plant bed by hand in rows, a busy time for all the family. We children dropped the plants and the men planted them with a hand planting peg. Later on as the tobacco grew, we worked each plant with a hilling hoe as daddy plowed with a mule drawn plow. Then came the time to pick the worms, called horn worms from it. No

24

pesticides were used then. After the top blooms had been broken out suckers would sprout between each leaf from the top to bottom. It had to be suckered each week until harvest time. That was such a hot dirty job, leaving black sticky wax on our hands. Tobacco harvest time was also one of the busiest times of the year. All the family pitched in and also neighbors helping each other. Every crop year was a new adventure always hoping for a better crop and looking forward to better prices. But for three consecutive years, 1930-33, there was very little rain and certainly no irrigation. Some farmers told of tobacco not bringing enough to pay fertilizer costs. There was no money to be had. Somehow we would get books by getting secondhand ones from other students and selling ours to others. We were never hungry though. Even during the drought years daddy was able to raise corn enough for hogs, mules, and also flour. The corn would be cut and shocked and that would be another time for neighbors to get together to have a corn shucking and the women would spend another morning together cooking another good meal for them.

We always had plenty of pork meat. Every farmer raised a pen of hogs and when the weather got cold enough they would help each other butcher and dress them. There was always a little friendly rivalry as to whose was the heaviest. Dad's were never second best. Good fresh liver was served for lunch on butchering days and some days later after the chitterlings and pig feet had soaked long enough to be cooked we would go to each other's homes for chitterling and pig feet suppers, those were great occasions for us children. Keep in mind there was no radio or TV, but we were never bored. We played games like hide and seek, , hop scotch, ball and when dark drove us in we enjoyed the adults spinning yarn around the fireplace.

Daddy always raised sorghum cane from which molasses was made. Granddaddy Elder owned a molasses mill and was called the best molasses maker of his day. That was another festive occasion when all the neighbors would get together. It was fun to watch as a mule or horse went round and round as the juice was pressed from the cane, running into a large pan to be cooked over fire. The mule or horse would have to be replaced often as they would become dizzy from the circular motion. Someone would dip the foam skimmings from the top as the juice cooked down to a syrup. Once mama's sister Emma fell into the skimming hole: ever after daddy affectionately called her "Skimmer".

One summer mama went to Hopewell for a short vacation with her sisters, Florine and Emma. Having been exposed to mumps before school closed, Evelyn and I had not come down with it. Mama had only been gone a few days when our jaws began to ache. Daddy realizing his complete responsibility, started administering generous dosages of castor oil to us. He told us all, "Do not write mama anything about the mumps, let her enjoy her stay." Polly obeyed only writing that Evelyn and Ruth were having a "swell" time – but of course mama got the message. Before the crash of 1929, mama's sister, Florine and her husband, Earl Harper and Emma and her husband, Claude Johnson, were living in Hopewell, all with good and secure employment at the Dupont Silk Mill. Mama, daddy and children went to visit them on our new car. Claude, eager to show us around, took us over (on our car) to see a bridge being constructed over the James River; as yet, with no side rails for protection. Claude drove up on the bridge, and had to turn around on it. I was afraid he would go over the side. In retrospect, I expect Claude could have just been trying to cope with having all of his relatives from Rolling Hill. That night for supper Emma had pork and beans and store-bought loaf bread, which I had never had before. What a treat! But their hey-day would soon end also, their jobs were soon terminated; the silk mill closed as did almost every other factory after the October crash. Emma came to grandmamas and granddaddys - I remember daddy carried her to Lynchburg, her going in every factory and place of business seeking employment. There was none to be had. They never returned to work in Hopewell and for some time lived in the Walker house on our farm with Claude working with daddy on the farm.

Another time for togetherness for the men around was wheat harvest time, with some using the hand cradle to cut it down, some bundled and tied it and others put the bundles in shocks to thoroughly dry in preparation for the day when it would be threshed. Daddy always found jobs for us - we children would go behind and glean any wheat that escaped the bundles. A neighbor, Tom Ramsey, would come with his threshing machine, what a beautiful sight to see the straw coming out of a chute into a stack which we later enjoyed playing on. The wheat would be taken by wagon to the mill and made into flour. Daddy always brought several barrels of flour at a time for our family and black families on the farm and also a barrel for a needy family of the community. Mama and daddy were always ready to share their material blessings with the less fortunate. A Psalm reads, "I have been young, and now I am old; yet have I not seen the righteous forsaken , nor his seed begging bread." (Psalms 34:25) Also, "Cast thy bread upon the waters: For thou shalt find it after many days". Now, at my 80-years, those promises often come to mind. The Lord has tremendously blessed us all in every way.

Carroll Carwile, brother-in-law
(with wheat cradle)

Luther Harper and his neighbors thrashing wheat (Hat Creek
Community, 1910)

Those summers were hot! No refrigeration for us but
Mr. Edd Wilbun on an adjoining farm had an ice pond and
icehouse. The pond would freeze over a foot or more thick,
then the men of the community would cut it up in blocks,

haul it up to the ice house. The pit underneath had been layered with oak leaves, the blocks of ice placed on them covered with another layer of oak leaves - - the ice to be used the next summer.

They said daddy was always the first and foremost man on the job and I'm sure he was; then he would get pneumonia from exposure. I vividly remember him coming in once after getting ice, lying on the fireplace hearth and mama wrapping him in quilts trying to warm his shaking body. He had double pneumonia that time. No one went to the hospital back then (or I didn't know any.) The doctor came, but with no antibiotics and other drugs, there was little he could do. They would use mustard poultices and putty like substance called Antiflo-gistine poultices applied to the chest. Neighbors came in and sat up with him at night. Especially do I remember Mr. Charlie Rush; he always was there to help. They always said the crucial or turning point of pneumonia was the ninth day. The fever would break or death would occur. Daddy almost didn't make it.

But the ice was good the next summer. when we wanted ice cream, my sister, Evelyn and I would go over with a burlap bag for ice. Mrs. Wilbun was never too busy to go down in the pit, roll back the oak leaves and get the ice for us. She would always say as we were leaving, "it's like a pig now, but will be like a hog before you get home." We didn't mind, mama was going to make delicious ice cream. We didn't have an ice cream freezer, only a tin bucket with a handle which we would turn back and forth in a pan of ice and salt. They don't make it that good now.

Ice water, and just to eat the ice, was a treat for us. In this age of germ awareness my son, Dr. Don Carwile, is astonished that we survived. I told him we washed it off!

There were plenty of blackberries, dewberries and huckleberries we would pick for food and for preserves. We would all peel and cut off apples and peaches to put on the housetop to dry to be used in winter for fried pies, etc., and served in cold milk.

Two or three cows furnished milk and butter for the family. We children did the milking, I believe I did the most of it. I didn't tell when I got to the house that the cow had switched her tail in the milk or as she had kicked at me, she had added a little more volume to the bucket of milk...oh well, straining the milk would take care of that.

We had a dazey churn, which was turned by hand. We sisters would take turns churning, turning 100 times each 'til the butter "came." The dazey churn now is an antique collector's item and very costly. I would gladly have given it away at that time.

BLACK EYE PEAS....Daddy always sowed black eye peas in the cornfield, not only for food but to fertilize the soil, the legume plants enriching it with nitrogen. In the fall the fields would be filled with dried peas, which we would have to pick when we came in from school. Daddy had a pea sheller and would shell the many bags of peas to be used for food in the winter and to be sowed again the next spring. I remember once a woman, Miss Gettie Garrett was staying with her niece and nephew, Mr. And Mrs. Bernard St. John, who were farming there at that time. Daddy hired Miss Gettie to pick some peas and with the money he paid her, she bought herself a winter coat. The sleeves needed to be shortened and I had become an accomplished seamstress by that time, so I thought. (I must have been 12 or 13 at that time.) so I volunteered my services. I cut off one sleeve, turned the coat over and cut the same sleeve off again! I was devastated, Miss Gettie had worked so long and hard. I had to do something!! I sewed the pieces back making such nice looking cuffs. She was so proud of the job I had done and of the extra touch on her sleeves. Believe me, I would not be telling it today but dear Miss Gettie has long been gone. It was also a valuable lesson for me in my years of making and altering clothes – always check before you cut!

HONEY....Another source of food was honey. Experienced men like Granddaddy Elder and his brother Uncle Joe, were experts in watching and tracking bees to trees, sometimes deep into the woods, where they were making honey. Then the men would go at night to cut the tree, a fun time for us. After smoking the bees out with cloth torches, they would cut out nice blocks of honey, some dark that was made from poplar blooms nectar, the white from sourwood blooms. One night Elbert Elder was cutting out the honey with a butcher's knife and a bee got on the back of his neck and he hit at it with the knife, leaving a lifelong scar.

CHICKEN...We had a small chicken house and in the spring several hens would "go to setting." Mama would put more eggs under her and in about three weeks, she would come off the nest proudly protecting her brood of some 15 to 18 chicks. We children were afraid of the feisty setting hens. Lee Lee said she would always get her mother to come down to her house and take the hens and chicks off the nest, which sometimes was necessary. We looked forward to the chicks getting to be "frying size", the only time we had fried chicken – certainly when the preacher would come. Occasionally mama would send us over to Mrs. Dick Johnson's, who ran a little store about two miles away with a hen to exchange for necessities such as soda and baking powder and we could have the remaining for candy, chewing gun, etc. How good were the lollipops. Once mama sent Evelyn and Norma Lee, mama's sister who was Evelyn's age, over to Mrs. Johnson's store with a some eggs to get a spool of thread which she needed. A family had just moved into the community; they had a handsome son whom all the girls around wanted to impress. Instead of getting the thread, they bought this handsome boy a can of pork and beans, that was the only excuse they could think of to come back by his house they now say. They still laugh about it and I might add, neither of them got Raymond.

Our sister, Charlotte, says once she and our sister, Rachel, got to Mrs. Johnson's store with their hen and the hen had suffocated in the bag; they had failed to make the necessary hole for the hen's head, perhaps the hen was already out of breath, having been run down by all of us, and then stuffed in the bag, in anticipation of the treat which was in store, but no candy for us that day!

Another means of barter for the young boys was the rabbits they would trap. They could get 25 cents each at Carter's store at Red House. Rabbits were also used for food at home, and possum hunting as sport, as well as a source of food. After they were put in a cage and cleansed for a few days, neighbors enjoyed being invited to a "possum supper" with all its trimmings.

Our mailbox was on Rolling Hill Road, which Uncle Mack and Lee Lee and our family shared together. It was seldom needed since there were no daily papers, no current bills, no telephone bills, and no magazines until later, "The Progressive Farmer." An added feature in going to the mailbox, Lee Lee would have a hot egg custard pie when we returned, which I think she would put in the oven when she saw us coming. We enjoyed the walk until we would see a snake across or near our grassy path – that order to Sears and Roebuck had to wait – back to the house we would go! When we put mail in the box two or three pennies were laid on the letter for postage and a green bush stuck in the box for a flag.

There was a man, Mr. Lee Snell, a politician, living in the community who would give us magazines to be cut and used for our schoolwork. Mr. Snell always brought his choice of candidates around electioneering. Mama and daddy respected his decision and then Mr. Snell would provide transportation at times for them to go to the polls. It was at Madisonville at that time.

At the present time, there are very few relatives and friends to whom I can turn for personal experience during the "Great Depression." Arie Daniel Elder later married my uncle, Len Elder, then living at Hat Creek recently told me this story. Her mother sent a hen to Hat Creek store one morning by her sister, Vera, who was on her way to Hat Creek School, to be exchanged for groceries that afternoon. The merchant told Vera that the hen had laid an egg during the day. She said, "I would like to deal it out in candy."

Most of the hams were traded also, mama and daddy taking them to Peaks store at Rough Creek and also Hat Creek store. They would get things like 100 pound bag of sugar at a time, tennis shoes for us, overalls for us to work in during the summer and cloth material by the yard to be made into our church and school dresses. Once mama and daddy went into the smokehouse to get the hams, which were hanging in paper bags. The largest one had been taken leaving the bag to appear full. Some minor offenses like that, and chicken stealing at times, were about the extent of crime in those days.

On the way to Grandmamas we would pass by Mr. Tom Ramsey's blacksmith shop. I can still see the red-hot coals and sparks flying as he beat out horseshoes on his anvil. Not under the spreading chestnut tree as Longfellow's poem goes, but under the cherry trees from which we would sample the fruit as we passed. We also passed that way walking to Red House School. Mrs. Ramsey would invite us in to warm. I remember her pinning my coat collar tightly up around my neck with a large safety pin before we continued on up the cold hill to the schoolhouse.

One morning as Evelyn and I were walking to school, Mr. Lee Snell walked into the highway from my grandparents house where he went for his meals, returning home after breakfast. About the time we got to him, he became ill and got down on his hands and knees. It scared me so much I said to Evelyn, "Let's go, we are late for school already." She said, "No, we can't leave Mr. Snell here like this." In a few minutes he recovered from a high blood pressure spell and was able to go on his way. I didn't think he could hear me and thought he was too far gone for us to help him anyway, so I didn't see any need for us to hang around wasting time. I became very interested in school all at once! Mr. Snell never forgot Evelyn's courage and valor and was nice enough not to remember mine.

Once he sent us all pen and pencil sets from Murphy's in Richmond while he was working in the General Assembly, where he worked each winter. I don't remember, but mine must have come before my showing such T.L.C. (Charlotte's memory of not sending mine at first: she had to later jolt his memory to send me one).

Another route we could take and a shorter one to go to school was through an adjoining farm belonging to Sam Walker. We avoided going that way most of the time and if we did we quietly went around in a grown up field making sure he didn't see us. We children had heard the story that Mr. Walker had ordered no Elder was allowed on his farm (our mother being an Elder.) This was because of an old family feud over farm boundary lines, so the story went. Mr. Walker, his sisters Miss Ann and Miss Fannie, neither married, lived a very secluded lifestyle, by this time only Sam lived there alone. One afternoon after we quietly passed to safety around his house, Mr. Walker called to us, "Tell your daddy to come over here, I think I have pneumonia." Of course daddy went over to Appomattox for the doctor. There again with no antibiotics, or other effective medication, Mr. Walker died.

I remember seeing him in his casket there in his log room back then with face under glass. I remember walking behind a wagon (probably dad's wagon) carrying his body far into the woods to rest in the family cemetery in a grave dug with pick and shovel by neighbors. Ironically, Granddaddy Elder helped dig the grave. That was my first encounter with death after which, whenever death has been referred to as "singing in the pines", and it truly was, this morbid flashback comes to mind. I still remember a few from Providence Baptist Church singing "Nearer my God to Thee", the pastor, probably Rev. Gordon, reading scripture and now, I realize, with no family to mourn his death.

The Walker farm, adjoining daddy's now was without an owner and as far as daddy knew, no heirs. Later as the old open cabin just sat there to be rummaged through, daddy searched through old papers and letters for any trace of kin. One address was an Oakley Walker in Oakland, California. Dad wrote to the address, and yes, Oakley was still living and with his sister, Bertha, (they too had never married.) After writing back and forth for some time, Mr. Walker was finally coming to Virginia to claim his farm. What an exciting time for us and especially the day he arrived in his Model A Ford "O Henry" he called it. He was a balding man, probably in his late 50's, outgoing, not at all like his withdrawn Virginia relatives. It was Easter time, he went to Appomattox and bought beautiful paper mache rabbits, colorful rubber balls and candy eggs for us. He told us about his candy factory in Oakland in which he had 100 girl employees. He said he always told new employees to eat all the candy they wanted. Soon they did not want any, he said. How I wished for that privilege!! Mr. Walker stayed a week before returning to California. I don't remember how much time elapsed before he came back. I do know at Christmas time he sent us a large box of candy, enough for mama to share with the neighborhood children. His candy factory was called "Home of MM Slim Jims" always on his business envelopes.

Tobacco cultivator   Rhoda Marston tieing
tobacco

Eventually he returned bringing his sister, Bertha, with him and built a small frame house on his farm with great expectations to grow "mums and pumpkins, probably an enterprise in California. Of course, that dream did not materialize. We always enjoyed him coming around, especially to the barn where we were working, his jovial personality as well as his help. Miss Bertha lived very much to herself. I don't remember what the relationship was to Sam Walker and sisters. She was a different looking little woman, wore red stockings which was odd in the area. Mr. Walker referred to her as the "ole girl."

The Roaring 20's

Ollie Harper and Eula Elder

Eula Elder, Ollie Harper, and Florine Elder

Ollie Harper and Elbert Elder

After some time they sold the farm to daddy and settled in Padukah, Kentucky, establishing a candy factory there. Clarence Elder from our community went to Padukah and worked in his factory for a while. Mama and daddy kept in touch and then no word. Later mama wrote to the postmaster of Padukah asking of their status - the answer was "deceased", thereby ending another chapter of my story. Later we were going through the house discarding old papers, there was a letter Miss Bertha had written to a friend back in California, while still here. In it she told of life in Virginia and that the people here were very primitive. We wondered how she could have concluded that idea.

Lee Lee said she went to classes in 1919 in Providence Baptist Church at Red House while the schoolhouse there was under construction. She said a Billy Collins who ran a store at Red House had a very mischievous son by the name of Joel. She said a hen was setting on some eggs down in a barn near the church about ready to hatch. Joel and several of the boys got the eggs from under the hen and carried them to his daddy's store. Mr. Collins being old and almost blind gave them the worth of the eggs in candy.

Another incident Lee Lee laughed and told about in her church schooling - she said she was the only girl in the class of several boys. She named James, Aubrey and Floyd Fleshman and Whit Harvey, the clown of the class. She said the bench was filled when she came in and she was looking around for a seat. She demonstrated how Whit Harvey patted his knee for her to sit on it. That in 1919 and in the church! She said, "Mama and daddy would have gotten me if I had."

Lee Lee told me that one night after she and Uncle Mack were married, they were returning from visiting friends over beyond Hammersly's store at Rolling Hill. Mr. and Mrs. Lou Hammersly and Miss Mattie Haily, Mrs. Hammersly's sister who lived with them had all passed away. Uncle Mack was going slowly to keep his car from getting muddy when all at once three haunts passed in front of them. She waited for Uncle Mack to mention it, finally he asked, "What was that?" She said, "Mr. and Mrs. Lou Hammersly and Miss Mattie Haily!" She said Mack forgot about muddying the car and put it in high gear. She said when they got home Uncle Mack wouldn't let her leave him in a room alone and she added "You can't tell me there are no such things as haunts, I saw them."

She also told of two buildings on their farm burning. Of course there was no fire department, no way to extinguish flames once they got started. One of the workers there had his girlfriend spending the night with him in the stable and they were smoking. Fortunately the mules were not in the stable at the time. Later, they also had a tobacco barn and the adjoining stripping room and tobacco sticks to burn while curing the tobacco. There was nothing to do but build again.

I also remember the same thing happening to daddy. He would sleep on a cot at the tobacco barn to keep the fires going when he was "killing it out." He awoke one night to the sound of flames in the barn. (1 of 5 barns on the road from our house.) Quietly he went to the house and told mama about it, not wanting to scare us children, he said. I remember seeing it burn to the ground; we were awakened somehow. That barn was replaced, too, by neighbors helping out. The logs were stacked and filled in between with a sticky mud made from red clay, the process called "daubing" the barn. Its endurance still amazes me.

Other than Mrs. Johnson's little store there was also another little store and post office about two or three miles away at Rolling Hill, owned and operated by Mr. and Mrs. Lou Hammersly. We children would walk there for a few necessary items. When the one-gallon can of kerosene (lamp oil) would get empty, we would go for more; if the babies were sick and "running a fever" off to Rolling Hill we would go for Fletchers Castoria and Black Draught, which was given to us in black coffee as a laxative - the cure was worse than the cause as I remember. I can still see a bearded

Mr. Hammersly as he scooped brown sugar out of a bin and weighed it and getting large, loose cookies from a showcase, which he would sometimes divide one among us children. They just don't make them as good now!

Mr. and Mrs. Mcfee also lived on an adjoining farm, whom I have always remembered with love and affection. She would come by our house and ask mama if I could walk with her to Rolling Hill. I would try to decide all the way down to the store, did I want candy or did I want chewing gum. I knew the moment of decision would come when she would ask me the important question.

We enjoyed visiting them, too. Mrs. Mcfee would make sugar cookies for us. I can visualize her now working them in a large bread tray. In my eighty years the like of which I have never eaten - the texture, the combination of flavoring and spices - predominately nutmeg and the best part, the abundant amount. I feel very fortunate to now own that same wooden bread tray which she used. Mr. Mcfee had scooped it out of a log in his wood working shop. Mama owned it after their death making bread for us and eventually giving it to me. Once Mrs. Mcfee brought me a mug of candy drops. On the mug was the inscription, "Remember Me." It was on the mantel for a long time but eventually it was broken. Mr. Mcfee also made three beautiful stools for Polly, Evelyn and me in his shop, graduating in size - they too, are only here in memory. The thing that fascinated me most at the Mcfee house was watching from their back porch as they would send a bucket down a hill on a rope to the spring below their house, the bucket would dip water and then by turning a wheel on the porch, the bucket would come back full of water. A "water boy" it was called. How I wished for that modern convenience - we had to draw water from a well in our back yard.

There had been a rift between the Walker and Mcfee families somewhere down the line as there had been between the Elders and Walkers, which had not been healed. The problem as the story goes, the Mcfees invited the Walkers to a chicken supper. Later they learned that the delicious chicken supper had actually been a crow supper. It seems for several generations there was still a "crow to be picked." So far, as I know, it was never healed - quite typical of the continuing prejudice between some families of that era.

Dresser: made by John Dabney Howard, mirror removed and replaced with shelves by James Arrington, refinished by Charlotte Arrington.

Wooden bread tray made by Mr. Mcfee

Christmas Memories

Christmas was a special time that we thought would never come. All year long we were on the alert for a box which we could set for Santa to fill. While we were working in tobacco during the summer we were promising ourselves that we would save some of the Christmas candy for times like that. On Christmas eve, before going to bed, we would line up our boxes around the fireplace and stay awake most of the night, waiting for daddy to come to the foot of the stairs and call us to come down. How happy we were. Santa was always so generous to us - I would get things like tea sets, a doll, jumping rope, water colors, small broom, and of course candy, sugar plums, an orange or two and the all important squibs (fireworks) and sparklers. If Christmas fell on a Sunday, mama and daddy would not allow us to shoot them; that took a lot of the excitement away. Once I didn't turn a squib loose in time and I suffered with a burned thumb all day.

Mama was real good at hiding Santa's gifts beforehand but twice I remember Evelyn and I found them, once in the stable loft and another time over the woodshed - of course, we were very surprised to see them Christmas morning. I wonder now how mama could get around shopping for all of us. Even though money was never plentiful, mama was never a "scrooge" with her family or anyone else.

Our Christmas tree would be one that we had joyously walked for miles, there on the farm to find, a cedar just the right size, shape, and color. We would chop it down and decorate it with homemade decorations; tin foil (which we had picked up along the way from chewing gum and cigarette wrappers) wrapped tack balls from a sycamore tree, colored paper chains and small pieces of cotton to resemble snowflakes. The smell of fresh cedar is still the smell of Christmas to me!! Christmas programs at church were also such happy occasions.

Chapter 3

Education

Attending Red House Elementary School played a major role in our early years of growing up - mine from grades one through six. It was a white painted wooden structure with high steps leading up to a porch on front, two classrooms, a hallway with a piano and a stage for free entertainment where we would perform often and at times for the parents. My special act, dancing the "Charleston," a rage of the 20's.

When the bell would ring we would form two straight lines, one for each room and when I say straight, that it had to be; each teacher eyeing a straight line from front to back. After making sure we were all in line and no misbehaving like chewing gum, and talking, we would march in to the tune of Miss Mae Pugh playing "Alexander's Ragtime Band" on an old beaten up piano. Then we would have chapel around the piano with us singing songs like "Mine Eyes have Seen the Glory" and all praying in unison The Lord's Prayer. Miss Annie Lee Sprinkle almost invariably would read from the Psalms especially the 1st Psalm, Blessed is the man that walketh... from the King James version, the only version we knew in that day. In my opinion it still far surpasses all others in beauty and majesty, and has been such a source of comfort and help in sustaining me through life threatening and lonely times, on hospital beds, also in periods of grief and sorrow from the loss of loved ones. How grateful we should be for God-fearing teachers and parents of any age.

Materialism was not the priority - the code of dress among the pupils was not set by the school authorities but it was primarily the same – suspender overalls for the boys and homemade dresses for the girls. Pants for females did not come on the scene until the mid 40's and then slowly - the first that I remember was a WW II war bride arriving in pants to meet her in-laws. We judged her immediately.

Lunchtime consisted of each pupil opening up a tin lunch box if they had one, if not, maybe an oatmeal box with homemade biscuits with maybe a sausage cake on it, baked sweet potatoes and sometimes molasses cookies, each of us eating at our desk. I can still smell the tin box as I removed the tightly sealed lid, which had been closed all morning. No wonder we headed straight to the warming closet of the Home Comfort wood stove after walking several miles from school, for another baked sweet potato. Sometimes part or all of the lunch would be missing. There were those who didn't bring lunch or couldn't afford it and even in those crime free days, "lunch stealing" was not uncommon.

One day Evelyn and I opened our lunch box, which we shared together, and no lunch was there. Miss Sprinkle walked to her boarding place for her lunch each day and when she returned to school Mrs. Carter had sent lunch for us. I don't remember what else it consisted of but there were two slices of coconut pie with a mountain of meringue on top. We hit the jackpot that day!!

In rough weather we wore goloshes over our shoes. Mine were always too tight, probably a hand-me-down from my older sister, Evelyn. My teachers, Miss Clara Snell, and later Miss Annie Lee Sprinkle, would spend a lot of time and energy tugging and pulling and fastening the many buckles preparing me for the long walk home, but I never heard a complaint from them. Maybe the reason for the tightness over my shoes was their thickness after they had been half-soled several times, by Granddaddy Marston who was a shoemaker by trade (50cents for repairing a pair.) He would put them on a last and nail more bottoms on them as long as there were uppers.

When I started to school I had already visited the classroom a lot before beginning first grade. If mama wanted to go somewhere for the day she would let me go to school with Polly and Evelyn and from those experiences, and learning from my sisters, I had already learned the basics. By the time I was entering the second grade, Miss Sprinkle thought I should skip and go on into the 3rd. She had made all arrangements to do that when one day Mr. R. W. Bobbit, Superintendent of Charlotte County Schools visited the school, which he often did, and Miss Sprinkle told him of her plans for me. I remember him looking down, jiggling coins in his pocket, as was his usual mannerism, saying, "She is too little even for the 2nd grade. That was it - no big promotion for me that day. Mr. Bobbit ruled with an "iron hand," whipping even big boys for truancy, etc. or if one became unruly in any way. (How times have changed.)

May Day was a grand event at Red House School. The boys would erect a May pole with colorful streamers and we would dance around it each carrying their own streamer. There was a jumping pole over a landing space covered with sawdust, rope jumping, all witnessed by our parents. White tablecloths were spread out on the ground for lunch. How we did enjoy mama and daddy being there with us. Evelyn and I especially enjoyed the relish sandwiches.

One fall, a teacher, Miss Jane Powell, a very timid young girl, came from North Carolina, having no idea what she was facing. Several boys, very large for their age, saw from the beginning that they could take advantage of her and they did. They would jump out of the window, leaving the classroom, disrupting in any way they could. She finally gave up and left. Mr. Bobbit sent Mrs. Lila Fleshman to take Miss Powell's room. It didn't take long to know who was in control. A day or so later, I was leaning out of my desk talking to someone and she said, "Ruth, get back in your seat." Thinking she had not yet learned exactly where my desk was I replied, "I'm in my seat." For that, she said, "You stay in after school and write, I must not talk back to the teacher 25 times." Between sobbing and crying, I finally finished and she carried me home in her car. Luckily, daddy was not around at the time or "25 times" would have been just the beginning.

Miss Mae Pugh, my third grade teacher, besides being a good teacher, on Friday afternoons just before closing, she would ask two of the boys to go out and bring in the boxes that were in the turtle-shell of her car. What a thrill that was; we knew we were in for a treat. Then she would go up and down the aisles putting something of each kind of candy, chewing gum, etc. on each desk. When she finished, we would all have a bag of goodies.

I remember once being very jealous when a girl in my class wore a new red checked dress with a beautiful black patent leather belt to school and she told me that Miss Pugh had given it to her. I didn't realize then the reason for it - truly she was a teacher with a heart.

The boys would go every day for fresh water about one-half mile up to the Baptist parsonage. There was a crab apple tree along the way. We would ask them to bring us apples back. My jaws ache when I think of them. The boys wore bib overalls and work shoes so they were dressed for the job. These boys also had to go into the woods for kindling and fuel for the wood heaters. I wonder now how they ever got through Red House School with getting wood, water, and making fires in the wood stoves, but my classmates, most of whom are deceased, all led successful lives. Three lost their lives during World War 11; Dewey Mitchell, Winiford Rush and Henry Easley Giles. As of now only Roger Pillow, D. C. Giles, Bert Reynolds, Lewis Elder, and Otis Elder (who is now in a nursing home), now survive. Most of the girls, too, are deceased.

A Miss Richardson (name changed), a traveling school official was visiting Red House School one day as she was lecturing about something, we all got to laughing, hilariously, because she was so ugly we thought; perhaps the most homely looking woman we had ever seen. When she came back again, she demanded of Miss Sprinkle that we all line up and each one apologize to her, and we did. We didn't mind apologizing, but the hard part was to keep from laughing again, She hadn't gotten a bit better looking, I doubt if we could have passed a beauty contest ourselves!!!

D. C. Giles recently told me about his brother, William, now deceased, chasing the girls at Red House School to their outdoor toilet. The teacher told him she would punish anyone without a dress on that went down that toilet path again. The next day William carried his sister Annie's dress to school and put it on, chasing the girls again, but also staying within the teacher's law.

At our school, on the last day before Christmas holidays we would exchange gifts with the person with whom we had drawn names. The boys had brought in a cedar tree which we had decorated with hand made colored paper chains, flecks of white cotton balls, using any tin foil that we could find. There would be a few other gifts, maybe one for the teacher or a special friend. There was one girl, Annie, who would lavish herself with wrapped gifts, and I'm sure enjoying the prestige of hearing the teacher call her name as she passed the gifts out. All through the years, when we have bought something special for ourselves we would say, "This was to Annie from Annie". Just all in fun. Actually, she was a lovely girl.

Valentines Day, at our school, was a special day for us, also. Days ahead we would cover a brown box with colored paper with a slot in the top of the box in which to drop our valentines. We made beautiful ones from wallpaper books, using paste made with flour and water. Of course, it was always exciting when the teacher passed a valentine to me from a "special" boy in the class...one that I had secretly wished would remember me with his homemade valentine, and of course, there were plenty of valentines, "To Annie from Annie".

THE GREAT DEPRESSION

The Great Depression, until recently I had not known any historical facts about the depression, only my experience in our immediate area of life, so I consulted reliable sources for an answer. As I said the future looked bright until Herbert Hoover became our president in 1929. Congress raised tariffs on incoming goods to a high degree, then in response to U. S. raising their tariffs, many other countries acted likewise. This had a ravaging effect on worldwide trade. Many stock market holders sold their stock causing factories to close down, banks to fail, and many farmers to lose their farm land, but dad was fortunate enough to hold on to his. More than 1,000 economists petitioned Hoover to veto the bill, but he signed it anyway. With many foreign nations raising their tariffs also, the effect on trade was disastrous. Our country suffered the worst business crash in history, the stock market crash of October 29, 1929. In just one day desperate speculators sold 16,400,000 shares of stock, banks failed, factories shut down, and stores closed. - almost every business seemed paralyzed, millions of people lost every cent they owned. In 1933 Franklin D. Roosevelt became president. He established the CCC (Civil Conservation Corp.) for young men, employment in road building, forestry work and flood control. Then the Works

Progress Administration (WPA) in 1935 in which daddy found employment. I remember daddy getting up early while still dark, in all kinds of weather, putting a wooden body on his wagon, hitching his mules, Dinah and Adah, to it, heading for the deep rutted, almost impassible road which bordered our farm. All the neighborhood men, who were willing and able to work, took advantage of this WPA work, with picks and shovels, horses and wagons, bringing in flint rocks from the fields to fill in the ruts and hauling gray soil and sand to cover the rocks. Soil was pulled up on each side, rounding up the road which was the foundation for a country maintained road and finally, now, a nice paved one. Dad's wages were around $1.00 a day, and the same for the use of his wagon and mules. His hard working drive and ingenuity earned him the title and position of "Straw Boss", over a group of workers. Whether an increase in pay, I don't know. I do know "God giveth the increase" (1 Corinthians 3:6) for dad and mama in their later years were able to build a modest, but convenient, brick house up on this, then paved and well-traveled thoroughfare and by now worthy of a name, "Bear Creek Road". One of dad's favorite quotes was from Sam Walter Foss' poem, "Let me Live in the House by the Side of the road and be a Friend to Man". Daddy truly lived it as long as he was mentally capable, with both blacks and whites alike.

Tom Brokaw, our NBC news commentator calls them the "greatest Generation". He said they are the ones who survived the Great Depression and experienced the Second World War. They saved the free world from unthinkable catastrophe and knew personal sacrifice, which later generations have been spared –how true!!!

Watt and Mary
(their new home on the road)

The House By The Side Of The Road
By Sam Walter Foss

There are hermit souls that live withdrawn
In the place of their self-content;
There are souls like stars, that dwell apart,
In a fellowless firmament;
There are pioneer souls that blaze their paths
Where highways never ran—
But let me live by the side of the road
And be a friend to man.

Let me live in a house by the side of the road
Where the race of men go by—
The men who are good and the men who are bad,
As good and as bad as I.

I would not sit in the scorner's seat
Or hurl the cynic's ban—
Let me live in a house by the side of the road
And be a friend to man.

I see from my house by the side of the road,
By the side of the highway of life,
The men who press with the ardor of hope,
The men who are faint with the strife,
But I turn not away from their smiles nor their tears,
Both parts of an infinite plan—
Let me live in a house by the side of the road
And be a friend to man.

I know there are brook-gladdened meadows ahead,
And mountains of wearisome height;
That the road passes on through the long afternoon
And stretches away to the night.
And still I rejoice when the travelers rejoice,
And weep with the strangers that moan,
Nor live in my house by the side of the road
Like a man who dwells alone.

Let me live in a house by the side of the road
Where the race of men go by—
They are good, they are bad, they are weak, they are strong,
Wise, foolish—so am I.
Then why should I sit in the scorner's seat
Or hurl the cynic's ban?
Let me live in a house by the side of the road
And be a friend to man.

Submitted by: Nancy Jones

HOW WE COPED

The common house flies were every where, because of pig pens, livestock stables and outdoor toilets. With no window or door screens, they had complete range. When company was there for a meal, one of us children would keep the flies off the table with a peach tree branch. Waiting to eat was the hard part for me. I expect I was more eager to get to the table than were the flies. Then after eating, they would have to sit at the table and "spin a few yarns" before we could eat!! Sticky fly ribbon hung from everyone's ceiling, "Tangle Foot" - it was called.

A friend, Mildred Wooten, from Appomattox recently told me of an invention by her ingenious father. She said he made a hole in their dining table with a rod and spindle, leading up from a foot pedal, through the table, with a Sears Robucke catalog attached to it. The pages turned as he pedaled, thereby shooing the flies away. I'm sure he must have had perfect coordination in order to eat and pedal at the same time. Burning calories would be a great asset now, unheard of in that day. She said someone set the preserve stand in the path of the swirling catalog, scattering preserves everywhere and breaking what would now be a treasured antique preserve stand. I don't believe his invention ever reached the U.S.Patent Office.

Eventually insecticides DDT and Parithion became available, also screen for doors and windows came on the scene. Our sister, Polly, upon finishing Phillips Business College in Lynchburg, and from her first job, used her first pay check to screen in the back porch, doors and windows at home. That was great.

We looked forward to wheat threshing time to have fresh, fluffy straw to fill the bed ticks. Mama would sew yards of blue striped ticking together to fit the bed, leaving an opening in the center to add straw. Everyone around took advantage of the nice clean straw from the huge stack. Artistic hands could adjust and fluff it when making up the bed each day, leaving a smooth, pretty bed under hand-made quilts. Later straw ticks were slowly replaced by commercial mattresses, thin, though at first, they soon became a household luxury.

Aunt Pat

A few families had a feather tick, also , made of chicken feathers saved over the years We all had feather pillows. Aunt Pat Joy, dad's aunt, came to live with us after her husband's death and brought her feather tick with her. How I enjoyed sleeping with her on cold , winter nights, burrowing into it.

Evelyn

Lye soap was made from scraps of fat pork meat and old lard put through a cooking process with Red Devil Lye, in a wash pot in the backyard. A very accomplished art was being able to make lye soap of the right color, and consistency of which Granny Elder was one of the best. Lye soap was especially effective in cutting tobacco wax on denim overalls, dishwashing and most household cleaning. Every household had galvanized zinc wash tubs; wash water was heated on the kitchen wood stove or wash pots outside, a metal grooved washboard was used to scrub the clothes on. Every woman took pride in hanging out a "pretty wash" and still walking several miles to visit a neighbor in the afternoon. Evelyn and I enjoyed going down in Mrs. Wilbun's garden while she and mama visited, eating strawberries and gooseberries. Everyone picked cherries from the Wilbun's wax cherry trees in their back yard. In my 80-years, I've never seen any like them. The clothes were then taken in and ironed with flat irons heated on the wood cook stoves or in winter heated in front of the fireplace.

SALESMEN

Salesmen were always coming around, even though we lived far back on a rough farm road. One day a salesman, Mr. Henderson, from Brookneal came with an invention, which he said, would take the work out of washdays. It was a washboard with about two inch spiral wooden rollers placed one below the other on the board, replacing the usual metal grooved ones. Daddy, always eager to help mama, gave him three bushels of wheat for it. That washboard may have saved the back, but its rough wooden rollers worked havoc on the clothes – back to the old fashion one we went!!

Then, there was the Rawleigh man bringing his wares in a black suitcase things like Rawleigh salve, which was a cure all for everything from stubbed toes to cold sores and a liniment that would open up your head, he said, and it did – the pungent smell would all but knock it off!!!

The McNess man was always a welcome guest as he would give us chewing gum. One day, when he came, mama bought a box of tapioca from him. Daddy and Uncle Mack had gone to South Boston to take a load of tobacco to market and would be gone for the night, so Lee Lee and her children came over to spend the night with us. Mama made up a big kettle of the tapioca pudding and we all enjoyed the special dish for supper. Well, we were all up all night, vomiting and with diarrhea, even too sick to go to school the next day. When daddy came in from the tobacco market that day, he wanted to know what made us sick. One of the children feverishly said, "tapioca" – like us, daddy did not know anything about tapioca and probably thought it was something we had "caught" at school. I'm sure his first impulse was to start administering his old stand-by, Castor Oil. None of us have ever wanted tapioca since, but it probably was the amount we ate.

Daddy always brought us a bag of chocolate drops when he came from tobacco market. He would put them in his hip pocket and sit on them on the way home. Mashed or not, they were so good. There were fruit tree agents also, now, don't get me wrong, we always enjoyed any one coming around. One day when mama and daddy were away, Evelyn and I were playing an imaginary game, which we often did. She was imagining and telling me that she was expecting some of her rich relatives from New York to come visiting that day. About that time we saw a Model T. Ford come skipping down the road. When this tall, thin, almost ghostly looking man got out and came to the door, we were too tickled to hardly accept the fruit trees he was delivering to daddy. Now with Evelyn also in her eighties, we still enjoy her ready wit and good humor, which she has maintained throughout the years.

Another visitor to our home was the T. Roy Adams, tax collector for Charlotte County. I don't imagine daddy was so glad to see him, but we were as he always brought us chewing gum. I can see Charlotte going with him hand- in -hand to the field where daddy was working to collect the money. One day in the 30's as we were coming from Brookneal, we stopped by dad's brother, Uncle Orin's house at Hat Creek. He had just bought a Philco battery powered radio, the most amazing and the first I had seen, to hear the announcer talking and as I thought, he could hear daddy and Uncle Orin talking also. I was so embarrassed and wondered why they would continue to talk. I must have been comparing the radio to the telephone, which too, I was completely ignorant of. The telephone system did not come to our area until much later, maybe 1965. The extent of my knowledge of "canned" music had been Granny's gramophone, a windup table top victrola which played black cylinder records, ballads in song , like "Wreck of Old 97", "Little Mary Phagen". The cylinder records were more screechy than music.

Within a few days after hearing Uncle Orin's radio, a salesman, a Mr. Harvey from Appomattox came to our house selling the same kind of radio – a battery powered Philco. He knew the right time to strike, in the afternoon when we children had returned from school. He went down to the packing house where daddy was getting tobacco ready for market. Upon "striking while the iron was hot", with Uncle Orin's radio still on dad's mind, and our presence, soon Mr. Harvey made a sale. We were so happy! Aunt Nancy, the black nanny to us, wanted us to play, "The Old Rugged Cross" for her.

We especially enjoyed the "Grand Ole Opry" from Nashville on Saturday nights. Screechy Carwile singing with his guitar from Lynchburg station, the "Lum and Abner", "Amos and Andy" comedies and many others. Daddy too, enjoyed the evening news, the boxing with Joe Louis and Max Shmelling and others. I always enjoyed company coming in and the radio served as a drawing card for that, as we were the first in the community to have one. Refreshments were usually apples and popcorn balls.

Benny Marston (notice the cider mill)

Daddy had a cider mill and apples were always plentiful from our orchard. When in season we children would make cider and kept some freshly made, which we enjoyed with crispy fried pork meat, which also was plentiful. There was also a drink made from "beer seeds" and sorghum molasses. I don't know where we got the first start, but I do know they would multiply very rapidly in a jar of water and molasses. A neighbor could get a start with just a few seeds from another. I believe someone ordered the seeds from a magazine ad, which must have been a form of yeast. It made a delicious, tangy drink. Another drink was sassafras tea, hot or cold. We children would dig the sassafras roots from the fields and boil them on the wood stove. I liked hot tea the best of all.

Stick matches were available, but like every thing else, that was purchased with money, conserving was important. One way was to make lamplighters. I enjoyed helping Granny make them by rolling a magazine page and twisting each end. These were put in a vase on the mantle to be lit from the wood-burning fireplace in winter or from the cook stove in summer. It was fun to fill the vase with pretty lamp-lighters – such a great sense of accomplishment for me.

I did not witness the time of the going of one neighbor to another's house for a shovel of fire, but it had been recent enough for there still to be a popular saying when someone came for a short visit, "Did you come for a coal of fire"?

Once Polly and Evelyn went to Hopewell visiting relatives by bus during the "Yo-Yo" craze. They had seen people on the streets throwing them in all directions, so they bought one, maybe for ten cents. That one only had a cotton string on it, instead of the rubber band which they thought it should have, so they returned it and got their money back. Women were also making "Yo-Yo" bed spreads and pillows out of scraps left from dress making. Dolly Wilbun made an especially beautiful bed spread and matching pillow tops.

Maybe there was not a lot of outside entertainment, but people were always ready for fun and pulling friendly pranks on each other. Lee Lee told me one such story which must have happened around 1922 or '23. She said one night after she and Uncle Mack had gone to bed, someone knocked at their door around ten o'clock. Mack went to the door in the dark and a man said he was a neighbor, Aubrey Fleshman, and asked if he could spend the night, saying he was too tired from the walk after visiting relatives in Pamplin to continue. Mack told him that he would first have to fix the bed (Lee Lee said she had to stay in bed with Helen, the baby). Mack made up the bed and invited him in. Two came in, Henry and Cubitt Elder playing a prank on Mack. Lee Lee said Mack had put a white table cloth on the bed for a sheet. Probably the only sheet they owned, she said, was on their bed.

Eventually the economy eased enough for us to go into Lynchburg shopping at times. How I enjoyed going into the 5 and 10 stores, Kresges and Woolworth on Main Street, looking at the rings - beautiful diamonds and rubies under glass. They had camera booths we could go in and have our picture taken for about ten cents and if you wanted a tinted picture, a girl would smear a little water color on it for a few cents more. One day after being in Kresges, we went across the street to Leggetts Department Store, we stepped into the elevator and as we were riding up, we noticed that Benny (my brother) was smiling and posing. When we got off the elevator he asked, "when will we get them?" We then realized he thought the elevator was another camera booth. Benny still remembers that day.

Ryland

Ryland recalls another one of those early trips to Lynchburg with the family. He says they were at Kresges lunch counter on Main Street enjoying ice cream with mama, when all at once they heard the shrilly sound of an electric milk shake mixer behind the counter. Mama thinking the sound was coming from an ambulance siren and probably racing to an accident or to the hospital, started shaking her head, and in her usual compassionate voice saying, "Some Poor Soul". - Electricity did not come to rural Virginia until the late forties.

I remember as a child, visiting granddaddy and Grandmama Marston at Hat Creek was such a grand occasion for us with Mama and Daddy, and a surrey full of children. From their house we could walk to the homes of Uncle Elva, Uncle Orin, Aunt Cornelia Elder and Aunt Nannie Bentley. One Sunday as Mama and Daddy were leaving to go home, I begged to stay with Grandmama and Granddaddy untill they would return the next Sunday. They agreed, and I was fine until bedtime, then there was a quietness and solitude which I had never witnessed before – a genuine case of homesickness!! They pulled out the trundle bed from under theirs for me and we went to bed "with the chickens". The clock on the mantle with its pendulum swinging back and forth saying, "Tick-Tock – "Tick-Tock" was the most melancholy sound I'd ever heard. Of course, I had to endure until the next Sunday and, in secret, but now, with fond memories – Grandmama's good hoecakes and pear preserves, watching her churn in a wooden barrel churn that with a slight push would sway back and forth in its wooden frame, like rocking a cradle, until the butter came. Grandmama was a tiny woman who wore dark colored, ankle length dresses and hair that would reach the floor when she brushed it, which she wore in a bun on the back of her head. Of course, she was much too old for anything colorful or elaborate, she must have been all of 50-years of age at that time! In the mornings I would help her sweep the bare wooden floors with a round handmade broom, made from home grown broom cane, tightly bound together. I dusted the dresser with a bunch of turkey feathers. I now am privileged to own that same hand-made dresser, minus several thick coats of paint. They said it was made by a John Dabney Howard, a renowned furniture maker of the area in their day (*see page 29)*.

At around age ten or eleven, I was visiting Uncle Elva's and Aunt Beulah's home, they were away and Grandmama Marston, in her old age, was also there, Frances their daughter, my age, and I decided to have some fun with Grandmama. We put on long coats, and hats down on our faces, went down to the barn and got a bucket of potatoes. We came back, knocked on the door, Grandmama there alone, came to the door, we told her we were selling potatoes, showed her what nice ones we had at a very good price. At first, she was cordial, explaining that they had plenty of potatoes, and did not need any. But when we persisted, so relentlessly, that she buy some, she became very enraged, ordering us away from the door. Needless to say, we left!! When Uncle Elva and Aunt Beulah returned home, of course, she met them with the story about the old man and woman selling potatoes. When they wanted to know where Frances and I were at that time, we had to confess to them, but not to Grandmama. We didn't dare get her enraged again!!

Another source of food was hominy during the winter months, which Granny would also make. Using lye, a strong alkaline liquor obtained by running water through hickory wood ashes. The hickory wood ashes were obtained from under the meat in the smokehouse, which was cured by burning hickory wood. The lye drippings would "eat" the skin from the corn kernels. Granny would carry the corn through a long process of cooking it in a wash pot in the back yard, constantly changing the waters to dispel all lye and skin from the edible kernel until it was white and tender! It was delicious fried in pork gravy. Once we were over at Granny's and she had just finished making a pot of hominy, she gave us a water bucket full to carry with us home. The word was out and in everyone's conversation that this was the day that had been designated (by some demented person) that the Lord would be coming back to earth, Judgment Day as we called it. Why would Granny give us a bucket full of hominy, why so much I thought, when just enough for one more meal would be sufficient, since the end of time would be today. Even today, I get an eerie flashback relating Granny's home cooked hominy and that traumatic childhood experience.

A rare, but exciting time was when an airplane would pass over our house. Mama was usually the first to hear the unmistakable sound of one coming our way. Even if she was making bread, with dough on her hands, she would alert us and outside we would all go, shielding our eyes with our hand from the sun, trying to be the first to see it. Mama would always have some reason for it being in flight that day, like..."something is going on" and if there happened to be more than one, "they are fighting somewhere today" – Then we would go over to Grannys and the first question we would ask, "Did you all see the airplane that went over today, it passed right over our house". Norma Lee and they would have seen it also with the same prestigious claim that it had passed directly over theirs. The most spectacular of all air shows for us was the day we saw the German airship, "The Hindenburg" pass over. The Hindenburg, modeled after the Germans successful "Graf Zipplin" was headed to its destination, Lakehurst, New Jersey. We were in Granny's front yard; I have a very memorable and indelible impression of it looking like a long, gray balloon, gliding noiselessly through the sky. I was spellbound, almost in awe. Later we heard by radio that it had burst into flames while landing in Lakehurst, New Jersey; its hydrogen filled gas bag exploding, killing 36 persons. The German Hindenburg was the largest airship ever built – 803 feet long and 135 feet in diameter and was on its 36th flight across the Atlantic Ocean. History now tells me that the tragedy ended regular airship services from Germany. At a later time during the first of sky writing airplanes, I vividly recall another incident. One passed over our house leaving a trail of smoke behind. To us it was like writing in the sky – "Hand writing on the wall" so to speak, a message to be interpreted, so we thought, but beyond Daddy and us to decipher. We all got in Daddy's pick-up truck and over to Granddaddy we went. Daddy would at times seek Granddaddy's opinion on important issues and surely with this mysterious inscription in the sky, this was one of those times. Settling all our fears, "Just smoke from an airplane which had already passed" He said, "What a relief"! Later we heard that the inscription was a message to our neighbor from her pilot brother.

Although with no formal education, Granddaddy of strong, stalwart character and, I believe now, God-given wisdom was able to settle many issues of his time – like matters of the church (Providence Baptist) and community. Certainly, it was these atributes and not through any process of training through study, or instruction, that earned him the honorable position of Magistrate of Charlotte County.

Before electricity came to our area, no one could have indoor plumbing. Charlotte and her husband, James Arrington, bought a farm near Red House, soon after they married and built a house. Not yet finishing the outdoor toilet, only the pit for it had been dug. She said a traveling salesman came to her door, needing to use the bathroom, she explained that they had only dug the pit for the outdoor toilet, but he was welcome to go in the woods behind the house. He went in the woods, stayed a very long time, crawled down in the dug pit and used that, later they could see that he had a hard time crawling up the steep muddy walls.

Providence Baptist Church

Church played an important part in our growing up years. We would bathe in the kitchen in a long galvanized wash tub, put on our home-made Sunday dresses, file into the surrey drawn by Dinah and Adah and off to church we would go. Providence Baptist church was a one room wooden structure at Red House, about a two-mile drive for us; many times we walked. Beautiful oak trees shaded the building, also affording hitching posts for the mules and horses. Daddy always tied Dinah and Adah to the same tree. I marvel now that they waited so patiently, without "running away", their favorite past time. Maybe they, too, realized they should be on their best behavior. Daddy always made the fires in the two wood burning stoves, one on the women's side and one on the men's side. The pipes from the two connected in the center of the ceiling, up through the roof. (no building codes to pass) Daddy would carry kindling made of pine knots, and then add wood he had previously hauled. No one ever thought of monetary payments for such labor of love. All the men of the church would meet at times and clean up the debris in the oak grove. Attendance was low on those cold mornings, with only a few faithful families spasmodically coming in. Finally, someone would say, "I believe all are here that are coming, so we might as well start". Mr. Ed Mitchell, Uncle Mack Marston or others would read the Sunday School lesson Scripture. We would sing hymns like, "Bringing in the sheaves"; "Rescue the Perishing" with Mrs. Frankie Marshall at the old pump organ, leading the singing in a voice that seemed to burst her bulging throat. Frankie was a faithful member and a very attractive lady. For my early childhood Sunday School class, we would go to a corner of the sanctuary and the teacher, Miss Rosa Marshall, would draw a curtain around us. One morning Helen, our cousin, started crying as though she were suffocating to death. She finally, between sobs, said, "She pulled that old croak (cloak) around us". Miss Rosa always served us candy before starting the lesson. I don't remember, but I expect the candy helped to calm Helen's fears.

A preacher would come from Pamplin once a month. I really had to be on my best behavior that day! I had to sit on the men's side with daddy. We always enjoyed the revivals each summer, invariably held the second week in July, usually the hottest and driest week of the year. Hand-held fans were placed in the pews by Henderson's Funeral Home in Brookneal. This gracious gesture was a means of advertisement, I'm sure, but probably could have defeated their ultimate purpose to draw business, by placing these, maybe life-saving devises, within our reach. Besides the intense summer heat, the overcrowded sanctuary with chairs in the aisles created even more heat.

After early childhood our Sunday School Classes were held up in the balcony. Especially do I remember Mrs. Gay Chambers as my teacher, giving me a Bible for learning the Books of the Bible, tracing the journey's of Paul and his teaching and learning, many of the Psalms. Some of which I still remember. Mrs. Mary Baines still holds a dear place in my heart, in recent years I would visit her in the nursing home, in her alzheimers state she couldn't call my name, but would say something about church. Once her eyes lit up, "and you would do anything I asked you to do", that made my day!! She had the leadership ability that encouraged us to do. I can still hear Mr. Hale Mason, in his strong voice, as he taught the men's Bible Class down in the sanctuary, rising to the balcony from below. I am profoundly grateful for all of these experiences, for my parents, teachers and all who made it so. At that time, I thought Church was just a way of life for us. Ultimately, I now know it is the way of life, in a humble background such as ours, or in the more affluent ones of today.

The Baptist Association meeting was a big event at that time, lasting several days, with women carrying lunch to be eaten on a long table out under the trees. One special day stands out in my memory, going with Mama and Daddy to New Chapel Church at Rustburg to an association meeting, I don't remember anything about the speakers, business discussions, or even the lunch, only one thing stands out in my mind, they had a barrel of ice water on a stand out under the trees. The barrel had a spigot which I could turn and, a dipper hanging within reach....what more could I ask for on a hot, summer day! Never had I had such thirst quenching drink as that rare ice cold water. Turning the spigot was part of the enjoyment, too. I'm sure the many trips to the water barrel were also accompanied by frequent trips to the outdoor toilet, located in the woods behind the church.

At one time in the thirties, fingerwaves became very fashionable in hair styling. We learned to wave our own hair by using sugar water for waving lotion. One Sunday with the church doors and windows open, the buzzing flies soon joined us...even in singing, I'm sure. We were thankful for the hand-held fans that day. Needless to say, we didn't style our hair with sugar water before church any more.

Around age 12, we joined the church and were baptized a few miles from Red House on now, Highway 615, in a stream of water at Scott's bridge. Even in my eighties when we sing, "Shall We Gather at the River", my mind wanders back to that childhood scene of being immersed and hearing the strains of that beautiful old hymn as we came up out of the water. The ladies would then go up to the Scott's house and change into dry clothes. The men would go into the tobacco barn to change, daddy was in the barn and heard some unrehearsed preaching from the minister, when he accidentally bumped his head on a tobacco pole in the barn, the words he used were not included in his sermon the following Sunday.

Spencer Abbitt
Died: January 2001

Aunt Jane Abbitt

OUR BLACK FRIENDS
AND SEGREGATION

We grew up with blacks on the farm, working there with daddy. The first in my memory, was Uncle Bill Ransom, who lived alone in a cabin on the farm. What stands out most was seeing him cook ash cakes on the hearth and singing spirituals for us. Then Sam and Frances Hamlett and children Byrd and Jerry Bagby, and children: John Thomas, Elizabeth and Annie Belle, John William and Charlie Milton; Uncle Tom and Aunt Nancy Hill,and children: Jack, Elizabeth and Gertie. They were all like family to us. We loved them and they loved us – playing and working together. Jerry always called me "Baby Ruth", which made me feel special. Even so, segregation was all around us. As we walked up the road to Red House School, we would meet the black children going down the road to Rolling Hill School. One black boy stands out in my mind, a Forest by name, always mannerly with a ready, "Good Morning", carrying an armload of books.

I'm sure he did well wherever he went. (I later found out that he had moved to the Washington, DC area and had been successful in establishing a trucking business.)

Mama always had food for any who was hungry and I think this was general knowledge among the less fortunate. Sometimes on short notice, it didn't take mama long to fry a batch of fritters on the wood stove to be eaten with sorghum molasses, home cured meat and preserves, or anything else she had cooked. When daddy would come in from selling tobacco, he would bring the specialty of hamburger. He would also bring an extra package of hamburger to give to the black family. Lena, having known sure that daddy would not forget them, would watch for him to come home, then one of the children would come over saying, "Ma said, send the hamburger on." I will always be grateful for love and support of black friends who helped me along the way. We are all God's children.

"......God hath made of one blood all Nations of men, for to dwell on all the face of the earth." (Acts 17:28)

Later, in my own home, I invited an old black man who was working with my husband that day in to eat at the table with us. Having lived in a segregated society all of his life, he hesitated. I said, "Come on in, Walter, and eat with us, we will be eating together in heaven some day; I surely hope there will be eating there". With Eldridge, my husband, insisting, and repeating what I had said, he reluctantly came to the table. Revelation tells us there are two classes of people, those who have washed their robes in the Lamb's Blood and those who have not – only two classes and two destinies. Today, I'm sure Eldridge and Walter are together in Heaven and sharing God's Glory, equally, around His Great Throne.

IN CONCLUSION

Time, like an ever flowing stream, bears all its children home, with each generation leaving a legacy of progress to be carried on in this ever flowing stream of life. For that reason, dear readers, I have not compared memories of living in my world of yesteryear to any given era. The plateau of progress, like the proverbial tomorrow which never comes, can only be compared by each reader in his own time and place, with each generation leaving a legacy to be carried on in this continuing stream of life. "In My Wildest Dreams", I did not foresee in my youth, nor would I now in my 80's, attempt to predict what the future holds; how many, or the varieties of "apples" to be lowered, but, I do know... "It is written, Eye hath not seen, nor ear heard, neither have entered into the heart of man, the things which God hath prepared for them that love Him" (I Corinthians 2:9). Judging future progress by the past, I believe those promises hold true for this world as well as for the world to come.

Precious Memories

Watt and Mary's 60th
Wedding Anniversary

Watt and Mary Marston
seated at 60th Anniversary
Standing: Mack and Leona
Marston

(l. to r.) Benny Marston, Renneth Marston, Watt Marston, Mary Marston, Kenneth Marston, and Ryland Marston

(l. to r.) Evelyn Midkiff, Charlotte Arrington, Rachel Rice, Watt Marston, Mary Marston, Ruth Carwile, Christine Jenkins, and Polly Marshall

Providence Baptist Church
Mary and Watt Marston
Fall Homecoming of '76
(just weeks before Mary's death)

60th ANNIVERSARY — Mr. and Mrs. L. W. Marston of Red House were honored with reception afternoon of Dec. 29 in fellowship hall of Providence Baptist Church in celebration of their 60th wedding anniversary. Hosts for reception were their 10 children. Mrs. Marston is former Mary Elder, whose marriage to Mr. Marston took place Dec. 26, 1914 in Campbell County. Couple has 21 grandchildren and four great grandchildren.

Granny Elder at her woodpile

Eldridge, Don and Ruth Henry Elder

(front, l. to r.) Hilda Mitchell, Nancy Mae Marston, Watson
Lee Marston (shot at 12),
Benny Marston, (back, l. to r.) Charlotte, Marston, Rachel
Marston, Dean Marston,
Ann Johnson, and Thomas Marston

(Taken on steps of Madisonville School)
Watson Lee Marston, fourth on back row.

Don Carwile

Carwile Gets
MCV Degree

Young Farmer   Young Doctor

77

Don Carwile's Third Birthday Party

Virginia Mae Carwile, Scottie Carwile, Linda Elder, Ralph Dews, Marvin Arrington, Tilson Carwile, Kay Rice, Marilyn Adams, Ronnie Adams, Larry Dews, Ray Joy, Renneth Marston, Kenneth Marston, Rex Joy, Don Carwile, Coretta Joy, Earline Joy, and Joseline Joy (*some names may not be correct*)

Know your Doctor

Dr. and Mrs. Donald Carwile and son, Will

Dr. Donald Eldridge Carwile is one of six new doctors who have arrived at the Blackstone Family Practice Center this month to begin two years of residency training.

Born and raised in Brookneal, Va., Carwile received his B.S. in Chemistry from Hampden-Sydney College and earned his medical degree from Medical College of Virginia.

His hobbies include hunting, fishing and golfing. He is a member of the Presbyterian denomination.

His wife, Mary Dee Elder, was also born and raised in Brookneal, Va. She has earned a B.S. in Pharmacy from the Medical College of Virginia. Her hobbies include crocheting, arts and crafts, and refinishing furniture.

They have one son, Thomas William Carwile, II, who is almost five months old. They are living on Ridge Road in Blackstone.

Dr. Carwile, Dee, Will, Sara Ellen, and Mary Anna

Acknowledgement

I graciously express my appreciation to my relatives and friends for their support, prayers, photographs, and stories for this endeavor. May God bless each of you.

COME...JOURNEY WITH ME AS WE TRAVEL INTO A MORE PERSONAL AND PRIVATE ERA OF MY LIFE...AND, EVEN INTO MY YEARS WITH "THE LOVE OF MY LIFE" AND PRECIOUS FAMILY – THIS AND MORE IS REVEALED IN MY SECOND VOLUME OF "IN MY WILDEST DREAMS...AND MORE."

In My Wildest Dreams... and More

Eldridge Bryant Carwile
January 10, 1920 – March 14, 1982

Dedication

This book is dedicated to my late husband, Eldridge Bryant Carwile, the love of my life, who passed away March 14, 1982.

As a widow of 21 years, my abiding recollection of Eldridge's wisdom and profound judgment has helped sustain me in facing life's challenges alone.

After writing my book "In My Wildest Dreams" many requests have been for more, a sequel they say, a continuation of changes which I have experienced during the more than eight decades of my life. As I said in my first memoirs, I was born on a tobacco farm in Charlotte County of parents, Lewellyn Watson Marston and Mary Elder Marston on a Sunday, January 25, 1920. They say it was sleeting and snowing, much too rough for Dr. Luken to get there from Pamplin by horseback some 15 or 20 miles away so I was delivered by a black mid-wife, Cecelia Thornton. How fitting that I chose that snowy day to be ushered in: all through my childhood, and now living alone, nothing is more exciting or exhilarating for me than a beautiful snowfall.

This morning, January 3, 2002, I awoke to the first snowfall of the season, perhaps so invigorating and giving me the inspiration to write again. As I sit here alone, a widow of 20-years, looking out on a blanket of new fallen snow, how peaceful and serene as I watch the snowbirds (Juncos) at the feeder from my kitchen window. I'm reminded of God's natural gifts and instincts that incite men and all other animals to actions which are necessary for their guidance, preservation and development. How else did the little snowbirds find my feeder, their food on this the first snowy day of the year? Only by His divine guidance and mysterious order.

As snow covers the earth with its beauty, obscuring what could be unsightly surroundings, it also buffers distracting noises, making for a more peaceful and quiet environment. For one acquaintance, though, this quietness was not always good. Rev. John Cunningham, a blind preacher who once lived and served at the Presbyterian Children's Home in Lynchburg told us that he had no trouble getting around the place until it snowed, then his guidance which depended chiefly on his keen senses of hearing and touch were extremely distorted. The familiar became very unfamiliar to him when it snowed.

I was born the third daughter of my parents, Lewellyn Watson Marston and Mary Elizabeth Elder Marston, in a three-room cabin in Western Charlotte County, then called Rolling Hill, Virginia, after their moving from the Hat Creek community in Campbell County. Already there were two girls, Polly and Evelyn, then after me another sister, Christine. Needing more space, mama and daddy began building a house farther up the hill, large enough to accommodate the ever growing family – four bedrooms, living room, dining room, kitchen and two halls. I was three or four years of age as it was being constructed. I remember being up there one day while the carpenters were at work, one of the men was leaving for a walk in the woods, so I decided I would go with him, he promised to bring some huckleberries back for me if I would stay there. I can still see the huckleberry filled bushes that he brought back to me. (Suffer the little children!!!)

(Front row) Ruth Carwile and Polly Marshall (deceased); (Second row) Renneth Marston, Evelyn Ellyson, Charlotte Arrington, Kenneth Marston, Rachel Rice (Back Row) Ryland Marston and Benny Marston

Our house was a beautiful wood-frame structure, painted white, trimmed in green. Plenty room for the others to come....Rachel, Charlotte, Watson Lee, Benny, Ryland and twins, Renneth and Kenneth.

I guess what I liked best about our house was the wood burning fireplace, rock hearth and arch and the mantle which held the Bible on one end and clock on the other. After taking up the ashes we would white wash the hearth and arch and the andirons with a mud-like dirt from down on the creek bank. Aunt Nancy, our black nanny knew exactly where the best white dirt hole was located. The clay when mixed with water and then applied to the hot surfaces, how good and clean it did smell! Even the fire seemed to burn with a warmer, brighter glow, as the heat radiated throughout mama's and daddy's bedroom – our family sitting room. Aunt Nancy also knew exactly where to find the best dogwood "sweeps" which she used to make brush brooms for the yard.

Wood heaters were used in the other rooms, also a wood burning Home Comfort cook stove for the kitchen. Our job was to keep the wood boxes filled each day. Daddy always had wood slabs, which he had hauled from nearby sawmill and sawed up for us to pack in the wood shed during Thanksgiving break, our days "off" from school.

I attended Red House Elementary School from grade one through six, walking several miles in all kinds of weather. On snow days it was too rough to attend school, but not too rough for us to play out in it all day. We especially enjoyed it after freezing over, skating and sleigh riding. We didn't have sleds, but improvised with things around the farm like the back of an old buggy seat, which was curved just right, and with some using large pans. The hillside was perfect, starting from our front yard, going to the woods below. The walk back up was also fun in anticipation of another ride down. Luckily, even with hard spills, we never suffered a broken bone or injury in any way, in retrospect, there must have been a host of Guardian Angels watching over us. When we went in carrying a snowball to eat after holding it over the fire to give it the special smoke flavor, and how good was the snow cream.

Mama would have winnowed dried peas and had them cooking on the wood stove with pork meat which was always plentiful and hot baked sweet potatoes from the stove oven and with home churned butter – what a treat!!

We also enjoyed pork spare ribs and backbone, which they had put down in salt water earlier at butchering time; its preservation still amazes me. There were no grocery stores from which to buy fresh meat and certainly no refrigeration. Mama knew just the right amount of salt to use with an exact amount of water to cover, pressing the meat down in a large stone crock. This was kept down in the old (cold) house where we had moved from. I think I was the only one mama ever sent down to get the meat out of the cold salty water – with my bare hands!! Then mama would soak the salt out and boil the meat on top of the wood stove. I can still smell the tantalizing aroma as we came in hungry from a day of play or from the long walk from school. They also had a special way of preserving pork sausage – after grinding lean cuts of pork, adding just the right amount of fat, salt, sage, red and black pepper, it was packed in bags which had been made from white domestic cloth, probably holding two or three pounds each. The filled bags were then dipped in hot lard, thus sealing it to be hung out in the cold smoke house to be used during the winter months. I remember its special aroma winding its way up the stairwell to our bedrooms where we were snuggled in, giving us the incentive to face the cold, run down to the kitchen for mama's sausage and those special biscuits. Even to this day, in my opinion, those biscuits have never been duplicated!! – And whatever happened to the Magic Yeast then used for rolls? It was a hard compressed cake which would keep on the shelf until ready for use. Mama would put the cake in a jar of water with potatoes, set it in the warming closet of our Home Comfort cook stove or in front of the fireplace to "work" in cold weather. She would make rolls that would rise to the top of deep bread pans. I have not tasted any truly yeasty bread since. That bread served with churned butter, what more could be desired unless it was to add some sorghum molasses or huckleberry preserves – and how about cornmeal mush? I think now the popular grits would be on the same order – mama would make a big kettle of mush and when eaten in a bowl of cold milk was so good. We always had milk and butter, but Dainese Howard now tells me of cows drying up during the drought and depression days of 1930-33.

Our several mile walk to school was also togetherness, and now fond memories for us. There were no long pants, but there were cotton knit union suits, long stockings and arctic overshoes with metal buckles which fastened from bottom to top for the girls. Even so, we would be extremely cold after facing the north wind on those cold hills. By the time we reached school, the larger boys had a fire started in the pot -bellied stove with wood they had brought in from trees behind the school house. We would all gather around it, the old stove taking its own good time to heat. Two of the boys, Otis and Lacy Elder would sometimes bring a bucket of fire coals with them from home. They, too, must have been under His providential care.

We like all children, enjoyed times when our parents would come to school for our special presentations. My specialty was dancing the "Charleston" – a rage of the 20's and reciting poetry. I was also privileged to get out of our limited surroundings at times, representing my class in spelling bees which were sponsored by the Richmond Times Dispatch at Charlotte Court House High School. I still indelibly remember every word I missed; and also, participating in oral reading and public speaking contests which were held at Drakes Branch and Keysville or Charlotte Court House Schools which meant something like traveling abroad for me!! Once I remember each school was given a speech from George Washington's oratory collections which he made after the Revolutionary War in which history tells us that he did more to gain our freedom than any other person. He was then looking forward to a time of peace and tranquility and the possible end of all wars. I remember as a sixth grader

I was chosen from Red House Elementary School to deliver his address, a girl of small statue, standing before a large audience, proudly and confidently declaiming his speech which included Isaiah 2:4- "Nations shall beat their swords into plowshares and their spears into pruning hooks; nation shall not lift up their swords against nation, neither shall they learn war any more." Little did George Washington foresee, I'm sure, nor could he have envisioned the horrific wars, which lay ahead for this, now free, and independent nation - Our United States of America!!- The Civil War, World War I, World War II, Vietnam War, Gulf War, and if the Civil War and if World I could not have shaken his confidence, surely World War II, the bloodiest of all wars would have!! How unaware, I too was, as I confidently proclaimed George Washington's words that I would witness the wars which were to come even in my lifetime. World War II, Korean and Vietnam War, the Gulf War, the Iraqi Freedom War, and the most horrific of all, the attack of September 11, 2001 - all of which I will refer to later.

As I said, school trips were rare opportunities for me to leave Red House, to say nothing of the new dresses mama would make for me to wear - one especially stands out. Once on short notice, I announced to mama when I got home from school that I was to represent my school in a spelling bee at Charlotte Court House the next day. She got busy and made me a tan pongee blouse and a brown printed jumper; I thought I was the most dressed up girl on the stage.

When I started to Madisonville High School in the seventh grade, I felt as though I were entering a large university, with students coming from far away places, like Cullen, Darlington Heights, and Pamplin. Madisonville was once called Chicken Town, because of the cock fights held there, my granddaddy always referred to it as "Chicken Town." I felt completely lost among so many strangers, my classmates. I was very small for my age, much smaller than those girls whom I thought had everything. Once, when someone made a remark about my size, my teacher, Miss Estelle Price, came to my rescue, "Precious things come in small packages", she said, thereby cheering me on in the midst of strangers. After a few days, a girl, Lois Shorter, soon became my bosom friend and from then on throughout grade eleven, she remained my friend, and we kept in touch until her death a few years ago, I lost a dear friend.

In spite of enjoyment of winter, spring was welcomed in by us with the daffodils or "buttercups" as we called them. How we patiently watched from our kitchen window for the field beyond our house to become a hillside of buttercup yellow!! How happy we were as we hurriedly ran down the hill on a carpet of fresh, green grass, that too, having been nourished by the winter snows. Then we would cross over a stream of peaceful flowing water, banked by scenic rocks.- even down in the woods, as far as the creek, "buttercup field" had spread its roots to its fertile banks. In awe, we would run all over the field, from one cluster to another, the largest and most beautiful buttercups being around some fallen chimney rocks, where an old log cabin once stood . Perhaps, they too, were proudly reflecting some precious memories from bygone days!!

When we had finally filled our arms with buttercups, reluctantly we would leave, still wanting more. Back up the grassy slopes we would go, inhaling their unique fragrance as we buried our face into theirs to show them to mama. We would put them in a jar of water in anticipation of carrying them to our teacher the next day. How beautiful they did look on her desk!! Classmates would often go with us home for a fun trip to "buttercup field". Even today, at 82, as I watch for the first signs of spring, there is a sudden burst of joy and hope from childhood memories as I inhale the fragrance and behold the beauty of the beloved and never-failing buttercup. "Buttercup Field" has spread its roots to all of our homes and to many others throughout the years.

Another anticipated time for us in the spring was getting to go barefoot. This had to be in the early morning, not in the hot afternoon, as we wanted to. The reason was something about already being acclimated or getting used to it as the day warmed up. How welcome was the green grass and the good earth to our feet! Later with the coming of summer, with daddy's help, we would dam up the creek for a swimming hole; how cool and refreshing was the splash after running down to it. But by late summer "freshets" usually had taken their toll, breaking the dam. By another summer we were ready to begin work on another. I am sure my grandchildren do not enjoy their many trips to various beaches more than we enjoyed our ponds and its scenic banks.

We also had our part of work on the farm, helping in the tobacco crop. One summer we and other families around broke sumac to carry to a market in Pamplin, a component from it to be used as a dye for shoes and other leather goods, they said. I don't remember anything about a big payment, but the chiggers have remained in my memory forever.

We also knew where to find the chinquapin bushes and the few remaining chestnut trees; but already an Asian blight had taken its toll on the towering American chestnut trees, which had dominated the East Coast, strangling them out of existence. Lumber from the American chestnut is legendary; rot resistant, straight, strong, excellent for everything from fence posts to fine furniture – the nuts also provided food for wildlife and livestock with farmers often turning their hogs loose in the woods to feed on the nuts. The American chestnut, tall and straight, could exceed 120 feet in height and ten feet in diameter, providing incredible timber. By the early 20's there were evidences all around of what had been the dominant chestnut tree – log houses, log barns, and rail fences bordering every farm. What had been the mighty chestnut, its remains lay felled to the ground, having succumbed to the deadly Asian blight. As children we played and walked up and down on them on our farm. Occasionally a log of chestnut timbers would reach the fireplace in our home; it would pop like fireworks as though, perhaps, in celebration of what had been a lifetime of usefulness, excelling in its dominance and legendary use. Sometimes a chestnut log would send out a bursting coal of fire into the room, that too, perhaps resounding its last attempt to carry on before fading into the distant future, to be lost forever. But now, it seems, maybe not forever!! Since I have been writing this, The Lynchburg News and Advance has printed a most informative and promising article about a possible future for the now almost extinct American chestnut tree. Through the efforts of two Virginia foresters, Fred Hebard of the American Chestnut Foundation and Bill Apperson of the Virginia Department of Forestry, the tree could stage a comeback.

Thirty years ago a farmer showed Fred Hebard, who lives near Abingdon, in Southwest, Virginia, sprouts rising from an old American chestnut stump. Now trying to restore it is his life's work, he says. Hebard tends 18,000 trees for the American Chestnut Foundation in his quest to restore it to eastern forests. Hebard's optimism is shared by Bill Apperson, who lives in Nelson County near Massies Mill. Through "Back-Crossing" much progress is being made. "Back -Crossing" means pollinating the American chestnut with Chinese varieties to get an American chestnut with Chinese resistance to blight. The American grows tall and straight, could exceed 120 feet in height and ten feet in diameter, seemingly clawing for the sky, whereas the Chinese chestnut is bushier with multiple branches, about like an apple tree instead of one big stem. The smaller nuts from the American tree are much tastier than the Chinese counterparts. "We're progressively diluting out the traits of the Chinese tree down to 15 parts American and one part Chinese" But some trees, like an old chestnut tree in Amherst County, known as the "Ross" tree were able to survive and live with the blight. Between one and seven American chestnut trees survived per county in both Virginia and West Virginia. (I do not know of any around here.) They are hopeful for at least the beginning of a comeback in the next 5 to 20 years. Apperson says, he feels like Jonas Salk must have felt when he was working on the polio vaccine. "It's really working, he says, it is in our grasp." I, too, am hopeful that I can once again savor a childhood delicacy, the tasty American chestnut and the chinquapin.... how about bringing back the huckleberries growing beneath them, I would say!! A friend, Lewis Elder, also in his 80's said, "Although the American chestnut towers above all other trees, strangely enough, lightening had never been known to strike one of them."

'We're progressively diluting out all the traits of the Chinese except for the blight resistance.'

**Fred Hebard
American Chesnut
Foundation**

Chestnut Rail Fence

Asian blight has hit this American chestnut tree. The blight has been infecting many of the trees since the beginning of the 1900s.

After reading my first book "In My Wildest Dreams" a friend, Mrs. Josie Ramsey, also in her eighties and growing up as we had, brought to memory some other customs of the depression days. She said, "when they were children they would roll and smoke their own rabbit tobacco cigarettes." (I don't know the scientific name, but rabbit tobacco was a weed from which they stripped the leaves to smoke. We too, smoked it a few times. She said, "they would also dip snuff. One day in school, she had a mouthful of snuff and the teacher asked her a question, she said as attempting to answer she blew snuff all over a boy sitting in front of her. Many elderly women dipped snuff back then, carrying it around in their apron pocket – some even chewed tobacco. Josie also reminded me of another childhood custom, that of getting chewing gum from the sweet gum trees, she said her brother would cut a notch in the trees and in the spring the gum would rise around the cut. We knew exactly where our sweet gum trees were; also, someone had cut notches through the bark, and in the spring the sap would rise, just the right consistency for chewing.

Black gum bushes were all around; a twig from them which we would chew the end soft, making a good toothbrush. We would ask mama to make the toothbrush soft by "tooshing" it for us, as we called it. We would all have bright shining teeth after the "tooshing" and brushing!

Life on the farm was not always work – one memory of amusement was when some men in the community formed a band going from house -to-house, playing what they called "music." Some had tin pans, some with combs blowing through paper, and one had a washboard – he being so conservative, shocked everyone when he went out and bought thimbles for every finger to play on it. I think he was the self appointed band director, also.

In spite of so many home remedies like Vicks salve accompanied with a warm flannel cloth for a chest cold, hog foot oil for irritated nasal cold sores, Budwell's emulsion for coughs, Fletcher's Castoria for the children's fever and the old standby, Castor oil, sometimes it was necessary for someone to go for the doctor, some 15 to 18 miles- not even a telephone in those days to call our family doctor. One neighbor woman, Mrs. Ed Wilburn, whose medical advice mama and daddy relied on was always ready and willing to come when needed. We would go running over for her when the younger children would come down with a fever or virus; she would always come, walking the mile or more in all kinds of weather, night or

Picture of Ed and Ora Wilburn
submitted by their daughter, Mrs. Dolly W. Taylor of
Urbanna, Va.

day!! I can still see that dear lady as she came around the chimney corner of our house, her head covered with a fur piece in winter, at times carrying a bouquet of winter jasmine, budding japonicas, and a few buttercups, from a sheltered corner of her fenced in yard. How our anxiety was calmed when she appeared, without a doubt, an angel among us. Mrs. Wilburn's, daughter-in-law, Rosa, said that all Jack, her husband, needed was to hear the rattle of the spoon in a glass of his mother's concoction and Jack's pains were immediately relieved. She had no formal training, but surely an honorable degree in TLC! Each spring all the children had to be "cleansed" with a dose of Calomel (whatever that was) So crucial was the correct dosage that Mrs. Wilburn was called on to administer it to us. After taking it, we were told explicitly not to get wet. Once after my dose, I was caught out in a sprinkle of rain, I knew then that my time had come!

Mr. and Mrs. Ed Wilburn, our wonderful neighbors, sent a mail order to Sears Roebuck and Company, but after much effort in trying to get the merchandise, and when that failed and not being able to retrieve their money, Mr. Wilburn boarded a train and off to New York he went, with one purpose in mind, to get the "jeans or the means", one or the other. I talked with their daughter, Dolly Wilburn Taylor, of Urbanna for some help in bringing my memory up to date and she said, "Oh, yes, but mama didn't want him to go, but he went anyway". He did get his money but never heard from the merchandise. Sometimes, now when I try to reach a living source in some business transaction and get only a recording – I, too, feel like "boarding a train," as Mr. Wilburn did!

Also when there were sick neighbors, mama and daddy would go over and sit up all night with them, as was the custom throughout the area. Daddy once came home with this story of one old man they had sat with who had been sick for awhile. A doctor from Pamplin, Dr. Luken, had been coming to see him each day; the old man thinking he was not improving as he should, decided he would change to another doctor, the one at Phenix. Daddy said he wondered how this old man would break the news of the change he was making to Dr. Luken when he made his next visit. Daddy, knowing the old man, said he knew that he would come up with something – but what? As Dr. Luken was leaving after his next visit, very weakly the old man said, "Doctor, you don't have to come any more, they say they are going to take me to the 'horsepital'." Now, hospital visits were almost unheard of in that day and that old man was not about to have one!! Daddy never got through laughing about that one!

"A Tragic Time"

Watson Lee Marston

There had been six girls in our family and three boys. Watson Lee, Benny and Ryland – when tragedy struck our family. Each spring an open air tent show came to Red House, staying about a week. Watson Lee had asked daddy to take him up to the show that night and daddy promised that he would on this, what started out to be just a normal cold April day. In the meantime a neighbor came over inviting the family to supper that night, but Watson Lee was still looking forward to the show of the year! Watson Lee, age twelve, seeing no reason he and Thomas, a cousin a few years older, could not ride their bikes up to the show, persuaded mamma and daddy to let him go. As he was leaving the yard, mamma called to him, he stopped his bike, I can still see him as he stood with one foot on the ground, looking back to hear mama say, "Watson Lee, don't get hurt up there tonight" - and his answer, "What is up there to hurt me?" He then went on excitedly, as this venture out was a first for him. That night, after the show, chilled as they were from being out in the open air, Thomas and Watson Lee went in the country store to warm by the wood heater – a store which was off limits for our family with its "on premises" license at that time for alcohol. The merchant, to be married the next day, was drinking beer and saying that he was celebrating his last free night, so witnesses said. He picked up his gun and shot randomly, a bullet hitting Watson Lee in his head as he sat on the counter warming before his anticipated bike ride home. Watson Lee died later that night in a Lynchburg Hospital as a very caring surgeon, Dr. Barksdale, was beginning to remove the bullet. Later the gunman told that he was shooting at a rat, but by-standers told differently. Words cannot describe the agony which hovered over our close-knit family during those dark days ahead. I can still see the tears as they drained down daddy's face, as we sat around the kitchen table, Watson Lee's vacant place at his side. Mama seemed to hold up better, somehow, as she tried to shield us all. Finally, one morning after breakfast, daddy bravely stood up and said, "I must go on for the sake of my family", as he seemed to conjure up the strength needed to go on. It has been said 'You can curse the darkness or you can light a candle'. Mama and daddy seemed to jointly light a candle, though at first with only a slight flicker; their light finally led us through those dark dismal days. The grief, and precious memories, of Watson Lee have never gone away, even 62 years later, mom's and dad's example of strength and faithfulness to their family has lived on to help and sustain us. Years later in almost unbearable grief and suffering after my husband's fatal heart attack, eventually I was able to follow their example, "I must go on for the sake of my family" – and now my prayer is, that this continued gift of strength and endurance be given to my family also, as they too, will face inevitable times of grief and sorrow.

Aunt Pat Joy, dad's aunt, came to live with us after her husband's death. She was a fine Christian with strict adherence to Biblical laws. One emphatically, she thought there should not be any ironing or pressing clothes on Sunday! We would take the flat iron off the wood stove and sneak up stairs out of her sight to press a dress for church - We loved her, and she loved us dearly, giving us much of her handwork - a beautiful knitted bedspread and many doilies, all of which she knitted on two bicycle spokes. I still cherish and enjoy them. She also, gave us many good Christian examples and Bible scriptures that we took more lightly in our younger years, but today as we are all older, we realize that her quality examples, wise sayings and experiences in life took on new meaning, have been good reminders and helpful to each one in the family. Many of her quotes come to mind as I am writing about her, but one in particular that I am often reminded is: "This life is only a dressing room for eternity" - what a realization that is now. Another, favorite Biblical quote of hers was "I had rather be a doorkeeper in the house of my Lord, than to dwell in the house of wickedness". This Scripture was also used in her funeral service.

Aunt Neely

Dad's sister, Cornelia Elder, was the colorful one! She also spent much time, in her later years, with mama and daddy. One day she was cooking with a pressure cooker on the stove, the gauge on the mark four meant danger – Renneth and Kenneth, old enough to see the pressure reaching the danger mark went running in another room to report it to Aunt Cornelia, saying "The pressure cooker is on four" – she thought they were saying "the pressure cooker is on the floor." I can hear her laughing now as she related that story. She also was a companion nurse to homebound patients in her old age. At one time staying with someone in Lynchburg, on a Sunday morning she walked to a church up the street from the patient's home – during the service she had a heart failure attack, becoming unconscious for awhile. Being alone, and no one there knowing her, or any relative to call, the people around her looked in her purse for an I.D., seeing her address as Brookneal, Virginia, some 30-miles away, when she came around, they asked her how she got there, she said, "I walked." I'm sure those around her thought there was more to Aunt Cornelia's condition than just her heart failure. She enjoyed, hilariously, telling that also. To know Aunt "Neely" was to love and enjoy her.

I have already written in my first book, "In My Wildest Dreams" of growing up in Providence Baptist Church at Red House. Many more memories and scenes still linger from there. One of an old gentleman, Mr. James Arrington (Grandfather of my brother-in-law) who when called on to pray, getting down on his knees (with no carpet on floors, then) taking him forever to get down and even longer to get up, so I thought. Also his correcting the preacher, Mr. William Black, once as he preached from the pulpit. Mr. Black said, "Money is the root of all evil" – Mr. Arrington, well versed in Bible Scripture, but probably only self-taught, boldly stood up and said, gesturing with his hand, "No-o-o, My Brother,

the scripture says, the LOVE of money is the root of all evil."
I Timothy 6:10

Mrs. Leona Marston with quadruplets, her great
grandchildren.
From left to right, Robert Donald Young, Ryan Andrews
Young, Mary Casper (Cassie) Young, and Riley Dillon Young.

One of my aunt Lee Lee's stories was about a woman
coming in church, sitting in front of her and Mary (my mother)
when they were young. She said the woman was wearing a
man's felt hat with the crown cut out and how she, Lee Lee,
embarrassed mama by laughing, so much that she got up
and moved across the aisle. Lee Lee said that she continued
laughing all through the service. Even after the loss of
her husband, Uncle Mack, a son Thomas Marston, and two
daughters, Helen Carwile and Nancy Mae Hamlett, and the
loss of three sisters and three brothers. Lee Lee's laughter
and humor sustained her and still did, even at 98-years of

age (A sad note: Lee Lee passed away the day before her 99th birthday, September, 2002).

Each summer large crowds would gather at churches for Association Meetings, continuing for several days, and at other times with lunch on the grounds. Some families would pack their lunch in trunks and bring them to church on horse drawn wagons. Recently, when I was telling my family about this particular custom of my childhood days, they were ready to call a halt to my memory stories and just chalk this one up as my imagination!! So in need of help, I called Beatrice Smith, age 91, to see if she could confirm it. "Oh Yes", Beatrice said, "My parents, Mr. and Mrs. Buck Nash, always loaded up their trunk with food and carried it to Midway Baptist Church for "lunch on the grounds". Then Beatrice checked with her neighbor, Ollie Harper Sublett, age 97, "Why, Certainly", she said, her parents' Mr. And Mrs. Bob Harper would use their trunk to carry food to Falling River Church, hauling it on a horse drawn wagon. The bottom of the trunk was used for hams, fried chicken, salt rising bread and such, with pies and other desserts placed in the tray of the trunk. Ollie says that very same trunk that her parents, Mr. and Mrs. Bob Harper, used is now owned by a family member, Mrs. Kathleen St. John (pictured below). If this old trunk could talk, it would say: "Maybe old trunks are not used to carry food to church now, but why not? Mrs. St. John, don't you know that trunks were made before plastic and certainly more durable, then I can return home and be used to store all important documents, pictures, even old blank checks and safe keeping of the deed to the family farm."- and, then I can be used again and again for "dinner on the grounds"!!!

George Washington, would you have believed this? Neither would I, wars and more wars.

THE CIVIL WAR: I have already referred to this war in my first book, "IN MY WILDEST DREAMS" ... but I would like to include a picture relating to it. The Civil War started on April 12, 1861 and ended April 9, 1865, when Confederate General Robert E. Lee surrendered his ragged, exhausted army to General Ulysses S. Grant at Appomattox Court House in Virginia. In terms of casualties, history tells us that the Civil War cost more than any other war, with 1,000,000 being killed or wounded.

FAMILY OF CONFEDERATE SOLDIER REPLACES HOMEMADE MARKER WITH GOVERNMENT HEADSTONE.

The family of Albert W. Marstin, a Private in Company A, 21st Regiment of the Virginia Infantry during the Civil War, replaced the old homemade headstone that marked his grave, with a new marble headstone, complements of the united States Government. The Confederate soldier was mustered into service on June 21, 1861, in Richmond. He died in 1862 at only 21, and left no wife or children behind. When his body was brought home from Charlottesville to be buried, his father, Eliphelet Marstin made a headstone from the soft stone found on the family property. After 126 years, the stone is almost illegible and broken off at the base, where the continual moisture from the ground made the stone soft.

"Gene Smith, who lives out at Hat Creek, looked up all the information about his service record and got copies sent to us from the government," R. E. Marstin, Jr., the great nephew of Albert Marstin said, "Gene also found out that we could get this headstone."

The headstone is standard government issue. It is 42 inches long, 13 inches wide, 4 inches thick, and weighs approximately 230 pounds. The family graveyard where Marstin is buried also contains the bodies of Chastain B. Clark, Christopher C. Clark, and Rufus C. Clark, who also died in the Civil War.

-copied from: The Union Star
April 13, 1988
MEMORIAL FOR CONFEDETATE SOLDIER:

Shown here after the new headstone was set up, are (front left to right) Ian Lacks , Jay Childrey, (back left to right) R.E. Marstin, Jr., Margaret Lacks, Earl Marstin, Mack Marstin, Polly Marshall and Eddie Lacks.

WORLD WAR I

On June 28, 1914, the Archduke of Austria, Francis Ferdinand and his wife, Sophia, were shot and killed by a Serbian sympathizer. Some years before Austria took over two provinces - Bosnia and Herzegovinia in which most of the people were Serbs, these people naturally preferred being ruled by Serbia, rather than by Austria because Archduke Feridinand was heir to the Austria throne. Austria claimed that the Serbian government had planned the murder. As a result Austria, Hungry and Serbia went to war dragging in almost every other country in the world. War was declared July 28, 1914.

The central powers, Austria, Hungary, Germany and the Ottoman Empire (now turkey) were at war with the Allies: Belgium, France, Great Britian, Russia and Serbia. Other countries soon joined, but President Woodrow declared that the United States would remain neutral, even after the Germans torpeoded the British liner, Lustania, killing 1,198 persons, 128 of them Americans. After so many sinkings of United States merchant ships, war was inevitable, on April 6, 1917, the United States declared war on Germany. Immediately all men between ages 21 to 30 were required to register for the draft. Uncle Elva Marstin, dad's brother, was among the first to go. The American forces under General John J. Pershing totaled 4,800,000. With the strong support of the Unites States navel forces in European waters to fight German submarines, the tide began to turn in favor of the allies.

Remembering that the French had supported the colonist in the Revolutionary war, Col. Charles E. Stanton, one of Pershings staff officers, upon visiting Lafayette's tomb said, "Lafayette, we are here" – History tells us of trenches that stretched miles across France, serving as living quarters for the troops, as well as first aid stations and supply centers. The mud filled trenches filled with rats, lice, flies and mice made life miserable for them. Uncle Elva told us of experiences while serving in France in trenches of extreme cold, a shortage of food, even dire hunger causing many to succumb. Once he said he was about to partake of his next meal, a cup of clear grease, when a German plane bombed their trench, causing him to lose his cup of grease as he ran for safety. Thousands had trench foot as result of the water and mud, causing the foot to blister and bleed, even in severe cases, the loss of the foot. Trench mouth was also an infection which was passed from one soldier to another by pulling draw strings of tobacco pouches by mouth.

THE FINAL YEAR , 1918

History tells us that the last Franco-American offensive of the war started September 26, 1918, with Pershing's First Army striking between the Meuse River and the Argonne Forest. At 5:00 a.m. on September 26, 1918, the first army encountered the toughest and costliest fightings Americans had yet witnessed in the war, lasting about six weeks. Pershing called it a victory for Americans, even though the German casualties totaled 100,000 and American loss was 117,000. 1,200,000 Americans fought in the Meuse-Argonne battle. About one in every ten was killed or wounded. Three brave young soldiers from Hat Creek Presbyterian Church, heroically gave their lives in this horrible Meuse -Argonne battle:

Lacy Carey- died September 28, 1918
Henry Lee Foster - died September 28, 1918
Courtney Berkley Bailey - died September 26, 1918

Courtney Berkley Bailey
Feb. 2, 1893 - September 26, 1918

Son of Lucy Mildred Bailey and John Yancey Bailey

Courtney Berkley Bailey, Private First Class, Company I, 317th Infantry, died with honor in service of his country on the 28th day of September, 1918, given at Washington, DC, Office of the Adjutant General of the Army this sixth day of June 1919.

Letters to his parent and pictures generously submitted by his niece, Mrs. Dorothy Adams Haley of Charlotte Court House, Va.

"Somewhere in France

My Dear Mother and Father,

I am writing you again to let you know I am getting on all O.K. I received two letters from you a few days ago. Now I want you to write at least once a week anyway, for it takes a good while to receive mail over here and I am always anxious to hear from home. I guess by this time several of the boys around there have gone to camp, so write me all the names that have gone.

How are the crops getting on, hope they have a good one and how was the crop of hay? That is one great crop over here. They have large hay crops and they do have pretty horses, their principal crop is hay, wheat, barley, rye, oats and potatoes. I was somewhat fooled in the girls, there are some very good looking ones but believe me, they are scarce. We are in the best place now, we can buy most anything to eat we want. We have been to places we couldn't, but can't tell you how long we will be here. We don't stay at one place long. There are most all nations represented here but Germans and probably some of them but we can't distinguish them from others.

Well, mama, I am going to close this time, will write again soon. Trusting all are real well from your far off soldier boy, with kisses.

Courtney B. Bailey"

Another letter he wrote was on Nov. 29, 1917 written on paper furnished by Army and Navy Young Men's Christian Association. In this letter he told about the good food he was given at Camp Lee. Some had measles and mumps. He wrote that Fernando Mason was in the hospital with mumps. He had heard from his sisters and they had sent a box of good food.

One letter he wrote was on May 22, 1918. They were preparing to leave Camp Lee in a few days. He told the ones here to sell his horse, as it was trouble for them to take care of it.

Some of the men with him in France were Fernando Mason, Hamlett Jennings, Edward Pillow, Will and Rob Baker.

In France

He wrote that he had been on the front line trenches and has been lucky and didn't get a scratch. We haven't had many casualties yet. One man in his squad had a piece of shrapnel to go through his kneecap, but think he is doing O.K. He is in base hospital.

He wrote about a girl "Elsie Janis". She had entertained them one Sunday afternoon. She was a fine actress and the first American lady I had seen. It certainly did me good to see and hear an American woman talk.

Marvin Berkley of Hat Creek told me that Courtney Berkley Bailey's mother, Lucy Mildred Bailey, upon receiving word of his death collapsed into a state of depression, just giving up, went to bed, and "never hit another tap" as he expressed it. Mrs. Lizzie Tucker, my husband, Eldridge Carwile's grandmother, nursed her in her home.

Henry L. Foster

Henry L. Foster was born in 1892 in Brookneal, Virginia. He was the son of Mr. and Mrs. Carey Foster. He was killed by a bomb in a trench during World War I in military service in France on September 28, 1918, at the age of twenty-six.

Mr. Foster served as a salesman in Myers Department Store in Brookneal, Virginia until his service in the United States Army.

Mr. Foster was the youngest elder chosen to serve in the Hat Creek Presbyterian Church in Brookneal, Virginia. He also served as a Sunday School teacher in the Hat Creek Church.

He was married to Pearl Henderson Foster, and was the father of Henry Lee Foster, a retired Baptist minister, who currently resides in St. Pauls, North Carolina.

Mr. Foster is buried in Arlington National Cemetery in Washington, D.C. Each year, Mrs. Pearl Foster, and her son, Henry Lee, would travel to Arlington for the Annual Memorial Day Services. The first year that they attended such a service, the Foster's son, Henry Lee, was only eight months old. Mrs. Foster and Henry Lee, now a retired minister, were able to hear speeches of five presidents, ranging from Wilson to Roosevelt at these annual services. One of Henry Lee Foster's memories of these services was that of Franklin D. Roosevelt as he rose to the podium for his speech, with the help of his aides, and a pair of crutches. He was quite impressed with the courage and determination of this great national leader.

(picture and write-up generously submitted by the Rev. Henry Lee Foster, II and his wife)

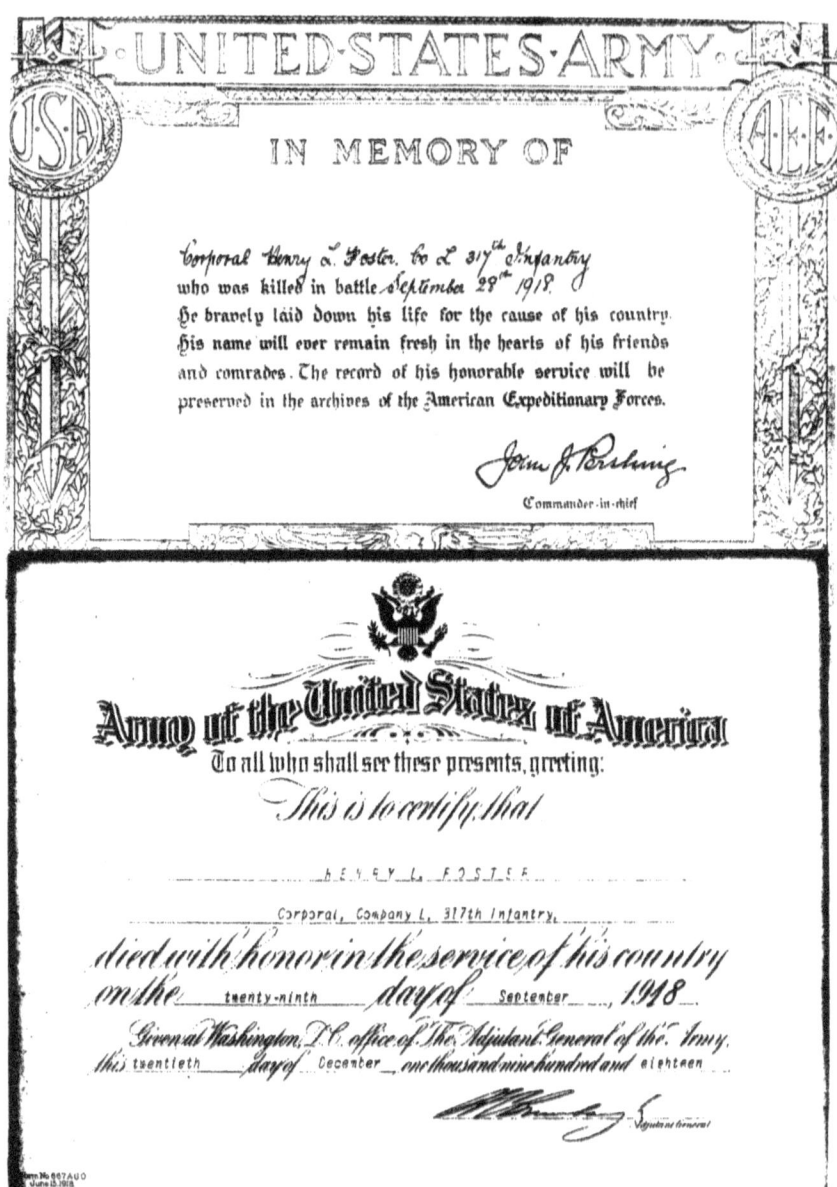

Picture of plaque which hangs in Hat Creek Presbyterian Church in memory of Lacy Carey, Henry Lee Foster and Courtney Berkley Bailey who gave their lives for our country in World WWI.

Picture of Lacy Carey, one of the four young men who left Hat Creek Presbyterian Church for military service during World War I. Lacy Carey was one of the three who courageously gave their lives for our country – all in the Meuse-Argonne Battle, France (September 28, 1918)

Robert Elva Marstin

Robert Elva Marstin, one of four young men who left Hat Creek Presbyterian Church for battle in France during World War I (to my knowledge). Elva was the only one of the four to return. He lived to see his son, R. E. Jr. serve in World War II and R. E. Marstin, III serve in the Vietnam War.

Pictured
R. E. Marstin, Sr.
R. E. Marstin, Jr.
R. E. Marstin, III

On the other hand, mutiny was disrupting the German troops as their food and supplies dwindled. In order to stop the revolt among them, Paul Von Hindenburg told Kaiser Wilhelm that Germany must seek an immediate armistice with the Allies. History tells us that on November 11, 1918, at 5:00 a.m., in a drizzling rain, German and Allies delegates met in Compeigne Forest in a railway car and armistices was signed: Ferdinand Fosh signed for the allies and Secretary of State, Matthias Erzberger signing for the Germans.

WORLD WAR I HAD ENDED!!

United States statistics: 116,516 dead
204,002 wounded
4,500 prisoners missing

History tells us that World War I did not solve world problems, it sowed the seeds that thrust the world into war again in 20 years, World War II.

WORLD WAR II

If World War I could not have been enough to shake George Washington's confidence of "No more wars...Nations not rising against Nations" surely World War II would have, or mine also, as a child, confidently declaiming his words.

World War II began on September 1, 1939, when Germany attached Poland, devastating Polish cities. After capturing Poland, in a short time they had also captured Luxembourg, Belgium, Denmark, Norway and the Netherlands, then on to Yugoslavia, Greece and then invaded Russia and Japan.

Japan wanting to expand in the Far East led the United States into war. About 7:55 a.m. on a Sunday morning, December 7, 1941, Japan dropped the first bomb on Pearl Harbor, with about 360 Japanese planes attacking the Pacific Fleet units at the Navel base. Fortunately for the United States, no aircraft carriers were tied up at the base at that time. After two hours of attack, the Pacific Fleet had lost the battleships: Arizona, California, Oklahoma and West Virginia and the tailet ship Utah. A total of 18 ships were sunk and all except the Arizona, California and Utah were later repaired and returned to service. 194 American planes were destroyed, four battleships, three cruisers and three destroyers damaged. There were 3,581 casualties. President Roosevelt called it "a day that would go down in infamy" On December 11, 1941, congress declared war on Japan and Italy after Japan and Italy had declared war on the United States. The attack on Pearl Harbor is called a "sneak attack" because when Japanese officials were talking peace in Washington, Pearl harbor was being bombed.

How well I remember that day, a Sunday, December 7, 1941, Eldridge (later my husband) and I had been to his church, Hat Creek Presbyterian in the morning and to his parents home for lunch. When I returned home that afternoon daddy met us at the door, distraught about the bombing that we would surely be at war. Immediately all eligible young men were drafted into service including Eldridge's brothers, Merle and Carroll Carwile into the Navy. Eldridge went to defense carpentry work on the Pentagon building in Arlington, Virginia, which was under construction at that time. The building, the largest in the world, houses the headquarters for the Department of Defense of the United States Government. Work began on it in September, 1941, and completed in 16 months, by January 1943, covering 29 acres.

There were so many good-byes, all eligible young men were drafted into service. Those from this area who did not return, courageously giving their lives were:

> Henry Easley Giles – died April 3, 1943
> Dewey Mitchell – died March 1, 1945
> Winford Rush – died March 27, 1945
> Deward Paulette – died Jan. 3, 1945
> Franklin Hill Elder – died March 6, 1945

On the home front all efforts were engaged as the men went to defense plants, building weapons, produced food, clothing, and carpenters building training camps. In no time factories converted from civilian to war production. The unites States, alone turned out 206,429 airplanes, 86,333 tanks and 11,000 ships. I remember every household gathered up everything in aluminum, old pots and pans to be picked up at designated places as aluminum was one important material that had to be imported.

Rationing became necessary on the home front, as urgent requirement for war materials continued. Items rationed included meats, butter, sugar, oils, coffee, shoes and gasoline. Books of ration stamps were issued to families, allowing them to buy limited amounts of such goods. Stamps for gasoline and sugar were very hot items, as I remember. Once I tried making a saccharin chocolate pie, but only once!! Even an old model car was almost impossible to buy.

General Dwight D. Eisenhower was selected as Supreme Commander. By June 1944, in an organized plan by the allies 3,000,000 men were assembled, 16,000,000 tons of ammunition and supplies, 5,000 large ships, 4,000 landing crafts and more than 10,000 aircraft had been assembled. A surprise attack on the Germans on the Normandy Coast of France was all on "GO". On June, 6, 1944, the first infantry and armored troops crossed a 50-mile front at 6:30 a.m. By July the First Army was able to sweep across France. Unconditional surrender of German forces came on May 7, 1945, a few days later, Hitler and his wife, Eva Baun committed suicide.

In 1945, the allies having cut off all communications to Japan, issued a declaration calling for Japan's surrender. With no response from them, the United States decided to use the newly developed atomic bomb. On August 6, 1945, a B-29, called the Enola Gay dropped the first atomic bomb ever used in warfare, destroying more than half of the city of Hiroshima. On August 9, another atomic bomb was dropped, destroying almost half of Nagasaki. The two attacks killed 70,000 persons and injured 100,000 others. On August 14, the Allies received a message from Japan accepting surrender from Japan. On September 2, 1945, aboard the battleship Missouri, the Allies and Japan signed the surrender agreements. General Douglas McAuthur signing for Allies and Foreign Minister Mamoru Shig Mitso for Japan. The U.S.S. Missouri, in which the surrender was signed now proudly stands guard over the grave of the sunken Arizona, symbols of triumph over defeat!!

President Harry S. Truman proclaimed September, 2, 1945 as victory over Japan Day – three years, eight months and 22 days after Japan bombed Pearl Harbor, World War II ended. What a great day of jubilation, with rejoicing and dancing in the streets was reported every where for families and friends of those returning, especially for the homecoming of my brothers-in-law, Merle and Carroll Carwile, both having served in the Navel Fleet. Yet a time of grief and sorrow for so many families of those who did not return, having given their lives for our country. History tells us that World War II killed more persons than any other war .

Pictures of Red House young men who gave their lives in
World War II.
Winford Jennings Rush (April 5, 1915 – March 27, 1945)
Dewey Mitchell (killed in Iwo Jima)
Henry Easley Giles

Winford Rush

April 5, 1915 – March 27, 1945

Killed In Philippines

Technician Winford J. Rush of Red House, Loses Life in Action Against Japs. Had Been Overseas Since 1940

Tec 5 Winford Jennings Rush, 29, youngest son of the late Mr. and Mrs. Charlie Rush of Red House, was killed in action on Luzon, March 27, 1945, according to a telegram received by his sister, Mrs. Joe H. Marshall of Lynchburg. The telegram stated as follows: "The Secretary of War desires me to express his deep regret that your brother, Tec 5 Winford J. Rush, was killed in action on Luzon 27 March 45, confirming letter follows. J. A. Ulio, the Adjutant General."

TEC 5 WINFORD J. RUSH

The last letter Mrs. Marshall received from her brother on April 6 was written March 26. She received the following letter from Lacy Ellter, a friend of Winford's written ... from the Philippines is ...

"Dear Miss Frankie:—The news came to me today at noon of Winford's death. Two of our best friends came to the camp here and told me about it. It was not easy on me, but as I am the only one here, I will do all I can to get all information possible. He is buried not far from here, and I will try and have a picture taken of the grave. I will also see about his things, although I know all of them will be sent home. There was a protestant service held by the chaplain at the cemetery. I spoke to the division chaplain a few minutes ago. He will assist me in providing you with all the details that you may wish to know. The last time I saw Winford was about one week ago. He had left his battery early that morning before eating breakfast. He was driving one lieutenant and three enlisted men down the line here. They all stopped by and I fixed their breakfast. All he cared for was coffee. Anyway we had coffee together, which we usually do while talking. I told him I would be up this week end to see him. He knew I would be leaving for home in a week or so. He told me to be sure and see him before I left. He had already asked me if I had your address so I could call you up. I feel the soldier that he was he would want you all to know he did his duty as he saw it and realized that things do not always work out as one would wish.

"The two buddies of his that I saw today want you all to know that there will be no one who will be quite the same, as we all had come a long way together.

"I feel I should write to all of you, but at the present will be too busy arranging transportation and time to do what little I can. So this can be considered to be to all who will miss him as we do.

"Well Miss Frankie guess I have told you all I know right now, so will stop for this time. You will hear from me again soon or else I will be seeing all of you."

Technician Rush was born April 5, 1915, in Appomattox County, Va. He enlisted in the service in December, 1936, and was at Fort Hoyle, Md., where he was with the Cavalry, when the above picture was taken. He re-enlisted in the Field Artillery and was sent to Hawaii in February, 1940. He was at Pearl Harbor at the time of the Japanese attack, and afterwards was sent from one Pacific island to another. He had not been home since going overseas, but had expected to be furloughed home in May.

Technician Rush was with the 25th Division of the 89th Field Artillery Battalion, and on March 19, 1945, his battalion received a commendation from the Colonel, Field Artillery Commanding, which stated in part: "On the night of 17th-18th March, 1945, the 89th Field Artillery Battalion displaced to forward positions in a manner to bring credit to the organization, the displacement involving a night march over difficult roads subject to enemy artillery fire and the occupation of positions in an area requiring a great deal of preparation. The move was completed in an expeditious manner and without loss despite the unfavorable conditions and shortage of transportation. This could have been accomplished only through the combined efforts of all officers and men. I desire to commend all members of the battalion for their excellent performance."

Surviving are the following brothers and sisters: Alfred H. Rush, Charlie S. Rush and Mrs. Alice Williamson of Red House; A. W. Rush, I. Harrison Rush, Mrs. H. M. Cumby and Mrs. Joe H. Marshall of Lynchburg; Willie Rush of Alexandria, and Mrs. Frank Armistead of Brookneal. R. F. D. Technician Rush was a nephew of the late L. W. Rush of Brookneal.

Casket of Winford Jennings Rush, April 5, 1915
Son of Charles Harrison and Rhoda Jennings Rush
Picture of casket and pallbearers provided by Janie Cumby Foster

Nephews (left to right)

John Henry Rush	son of	John Willie Rush
Jimmy Williamson	son of	Alice Mae Rush Williamson
Keith Armistead	son of	Isabelle Hall Armistead
Charles Cumby	son of	Florence Howard Rush Cumby
William Rush	son of	Aubrey Watkins Rush
Thornton Marshall	son of	Emma Frances Rush Marshall
Hugh Cumby	son of	Florence Howard Rush Cumby
Harry Cumby	son of	Florence Howard Rush Cumby

Picture of marker in family cemetery at Red House

Dewey Mitchell

Dewey Mitchell from Red House Baptist Church courageously gave his life for his country during World War II in the island of Iwo Jima. His sister, Hilda Mitchell Johnson of South Boston, Va. said that his body was so badly mangled by an enemy bombing that the remains were buried there. (Pictures generously submitted by Dewey's sister, Margaret Mitchell Peade of Hopewell, Va.)

Picture of Dewey and family in front of Mitchell home.
Front: Mr. Edd Mitchell (father), Mrs. Amanda Puckett
Mitchell (mother). Back: Margaret Mitchell Peade (sister),
Dewey Mitchell, Len Mitchell (brother), and Hilda Mitchell
Johnson (sister).

Len Mitchell (Dewey's brother) vividly described to me the heartrending account of the day the family received word of Dewey's death. Len said that he and Mrs. Mitchell were at work in the garden below the house when an official came to deliver the devastating message. That must be the most distressful word that any parents must endure. (I should know that Mrs. Mitchell this virtuous woman would be at work for her family.) Proverbs 31:10-31, "Who can find a virtuous woman?". Verse 27, "She looketh well to the ways of her household/and eateth not the bread of idleness." Mrs. Mitchell always had good food - her fresh vegetables - delightful hospitality - the same goes for Mr. Mitchell. How we enjoyed visiting there after church for Sunday lunch and they with us at other times.

Funeral Of Henry Giles Held At Red House Home

Sergeant Giles

Sergeant Giles Was Victim Of Fire At Dow Field In Maine

Brookneal, Jan. 19—Funeral services for Technical Sergeant Henry Easley Giles, who died early Wednesday morning at Dow Field, Bangor, Me., were conducted Sunday afternoon at 2:30 o'clock from the home of his parents, Mr. and Mrs. Yaple A. Giles, Red House, Campbell County, by Rev. W. M. Black of Pamplin, assisted by Rev. Robert S. Booker and Rev. Elton McDow II. A quartet from Brookneal sang several selections, and taps were sounded by B. F. Ginther, Jr.

Honorary pallbearers were Jack Woosley, Melvin Jefferson, Hanson Rush, Hugh Mitchell, Carey Jefferson, Carter Pankey, C. T. Moses, F. B. Jefferson, Alfred Rush, T. H. Chambers, Clyde Jackson, Joe Marshall, Charlie Rush, E. W. Mitchell, W. B. Renylands, Jack Wilbourne, R. E. Wilbourne, F. C. Guthrie, D. C. Jennings, J. F. Jennings, M. E. Jennings, James Fleshman, Clyde Fleshman, Aubrey Fleshman, Paul Bennett, Irving Jennings, J R. McGee, Robert Harris, Hampton Adams, I. R. Orcutt, W. E. Giles, Jim Williamson, Earl Bennett, Lewis Smith, L W. Marston and Joe Terry.

Flowers were carried by Irwin Orcutt, Evelyn Orcutt, Hilda Jefferson, Edna Jefferson, Marion Jefferson, Frances Snell, Ruth Marston, Rachel Marston, Mrs. O. B. Moorefield, Charlotte Marston, Mrs. W. R. Landrum, Mrs. Jack Wilbourne, Hilda Mitchell, Barbara Ann Giles, Josephine O'Conner and William McGee.

Active pallbearers were Willie Adams, Len Elder, Oscar Moorefield, Kermit Landrum, Roy Myers and Roger Pillow.

Technical Sergeant Henry Easley Giles courageously gave his life serving his country in the line of duty at Dow Field, Bangor, Maine. Pictures and write-up generously submitted by his brother, D. C. Giles of Lynchburg, Va.

PVT Franklin Hill Elder, a member of Beulah Baptist Church at Hat Creek who courageously gave his life for his country. Picture and write-up generously submitted by his sister, Mrs. Frances Elder Ward.

December 31, 1924 – March 6, 1945
Buried at Beulah Baptist Church with military rites.

Pvt. Franklin Elder Killed In Germany; Other Deaths

Soldier From Brookneal
Lost Life In Action
On March 6

Pvt. Franklin Hill Elder, 20, was killed in action in Germany, March 6, according to a telegram from the War Department received by his parents, Mr. and Mrs. Randolph T. Elder of Brookneal.

Pvt. Elder entered the Army March 24, 1944, at Fort Meade, Md. He trained at Camp Croft, S. C., and Camp McCoy, Wisc., and left for overseas duty last November.

Pvt. Elder was born December 31, 1924, in Campbell County. He was a member of the Beulah Baptist Church.

Besides his parents, Pvt. Elder is survived by 13 brothers and sisters: Pvt. Roy W. Elder, Camp Wheeler, Ga.; Pfc. Morris H. Elder, serving with the Army in Italy; Claude Elder of Union Hill; William Elder of Brookneal; Miss Josephine Elder of Lynchburg; Mrs. Raymond Ward of Brookneal; Mrs. Colgate Lipscomb of Aspen; Mrs. Junior St. John of Phenix; Miss Mary Love Elder, Miss Eunice Elder, Miss Gertrude Elder, Miss Justine Elder and Miss Nancy Elder, all of Brookneal.

Sergeant James Corbin Elder
*(Picture and information submitted by Jane Carolyn
Gleason, Corbin's daughter)*

Sergeant James Corbin Elder was a sergeant in Patton's 3rd
Army; 6th Armored Division; 44th Infantry Armored Battalion;

Technician 4th Grade. He did his basic training in Ft. Chaffee, Arkansas. He arrived on Normandy Beach a week after D-Day. He fought the entire Battle of the Bulge (December 1944 – January 1945). He said the warmest place to sleep was in the snow.

Actually, he refused to talk about what he went through and during the later years of his life, my husband pulled information out of him. Even then, he would break out in a sweat talking about it.

When the European war was over in May 1945, he was given shovels and masks and told to take his men to a place called Buchenwald. His was one of the first troops to arrive in this notorious concentration camp. He was given the Bronze Star for his bravery in liberating this camp and saving many lives.

Homecoming of my brothers-in-law, Merle and Carroll
Carwile
(Merle on right, Carroll on left)

Ruth Marston Carwile

VIETNAM

Vietnam vet relives war experiences through movie

Gene Smith

PAULA L. BRYANT
The Union Star Editor

Last month as Gene Smith of Brooknezi sat in a darkened theatre viewing the movie "We Were Soldiers," the Vietnam veteran was taken back in time some 37 years to the epochy la Drang Valley, the valley of death where the first major battle was fought.

"When I watched the movie, it really made me thankful that I'd made it through la Drang because a lot of people I knew didn't," said a humble Gene Smith as he recalled living through days in that "really eerie looking place."

Smith served in the First Battalion, 9th Air Cavalry Squadron during the early stages of the Vietnam Conflict, and he was there when that first major battle was fought.

"Our job was to provide reconnaissance for the 7th Cavalry to let them know what was coming," Smith said.

As he watched actor Mel Gibson accurately portray the respected character of Lt. General Harold Moore, Smith said he remembered well providing reconnaissance for Lt. Moore's division during the early stages of the war.

Smith personally knows the two main characters portrayed in the movie. Retired Lt. General Moore and Joseph Galloway, author of the book "We Were Soldiers" on which the movie is based, and have had opportunities to talk with them at reunions.

"It was just seeing his (Moore's) leadership style again and the style of the sergeant major portrayed in the movie that made me remember what a respected man Harold Moore was," Smith added.

According to Smith, actor Mel Gibson went and stayed with Moore and got to know him before making the movie in which he so accurately portrayed the leader's character.

"The movie was good, but some of the action scenes were not very accurate," Smith said explaining that the terrain looked quite a bit similar to that in Vietnam despite the fact the movie was filmed in California.

"The action scenes were pretty much Hollywood because you didn't usually see the enemy in combat like portrayed in the movie," he said explaining that most of the time, the enemy stayed hidden.

Smith explained the first North Vietnamese soldier he ever saw tried to surrender to his unit.

"The gunners wanted to shoot him, but I talked the pilot out of shooting him. We didn't pick him up though because we thought it was a trap. They'd do that," he said explaining that one would come out while the others remained hidden waiting to draw the Americans into the snare.

It was interesting about the battles," Smith said recalling one in particular when

Please see page 13

Vietnam

Continued from page 1

American soldiers had just been issued M-16s.

"When they dropped the Americans in there that morning, the Vietnamese were aggressive and attacked with large numbers of casualties.

"The Americans who weren't that experienced with the weapons were running out of ammunition because they had fired so many rounds on automatic."

After that learning experience, Smith said a regulation was passed that permitted only one or two men to fire their weapons on automatic, while the others had to fire on semi-automatic.

As he watched the scenes of the movie unfold, Smith said it brought back memories of buddies who were not as fortunate as himself.

"I knew some of the guys killed in that first major battle. My wingman's plane was shot down and captured. The North Vietnamese

took them out in the woods and executed them," Smith said. "We located their aircraft, but they were already dead."

Smith later would receive an air medal for heroism for going back to find his wingman's plane that was shot down in Vietnam in November, 1965.

"I thought more about the guys who left behind families back at Fort Benning, GA," he said remembering how taxi drivers would walk up to the door, knock on it and deliver that fateful telegram telling loved ones that their soldier had been killed.

And the la Drang Valley ran red with blood as lives were lost on both sides.

Towards the end of the battle, Smith recalled Americans conducting a massive B-52 bombing strike of the la Drang Valley.

"I thought nothing could've lived through that, and when they sent us down to recon after the bombing I

was in the third aircraft. I was amazed when North Vietnamese started shooting at us. I couldn't believe anyone could live through that bombing, but they did.

"Our gunners just started firing," Smith continued relating a personal incident that literally "branded" the memory in his mind as casings from the gunners' weapons literally filled the floor of the chopper.

"I had on a helmet, and a casing landed between my helmet and neck," Smith said recalling his screams for help which fell on deaf ears due to the noise of gun fire.

"It just sat there and sizzled on the back of my neck. It burned, and I was screaming for the other pilot to take the controls, but I just had to sit there and let it sizzle."

Smith said he was most impressed by the movie's portrayal of the soldiers' wives who were left behind at Fort Benning not knowing what to expect.

"They really got it right in the

movie the way the wives support each other and hung in there together."

As the movie came to an end, Smith said he was flooded with the same feeling he had in July 1966 when he left Vietnam.

"I was just so glad to be out of there and be able to eat cheeseburgers and sleep between clean sheets," Smith said.

And on a more deeper level, the movie left Smith with a sense of appreciation for having made it out at all.

"Quite a few of my buddies did n't make it back. My troop commander and troop executive office were killed, and my squadron executive officer also was killed on mission.

"I was at Plei Ku when they started bringing in the dead, and there were all these 19 and 20-year-old That was a sobering experience...just thinking it might be me."

TERRORIST ATTACK - SEPTEMBER 11, 2001

If the awful wars since George Washington's hope of "No More Wars", that I so proudly declaimed, as it was called then, would not have shocked his confidence, surely the horrific attacks of September 11, 2001, would have! I was in my kitchen frying chicken for a luncheon at my church, as I'm sure everyone else will remember where they were on that fateful day, when my brother, Kenneth Marston, called saying "Turn your television on, we are being bombed!!" Terrorist had bombed the World Trade Center in New York, the Pentagon in Washington, D. C., and Pan Am Flight 93 had crashed in Shanksville, Pennsylvania. Statistics say: 2,819 people died in the New York Trade Center and 343 firefighters lost their lives, costing 83 billion dollars in New York. 184 persons lost their lives in the Pentagon attack; 57 of the number were on the plane also piloted by a suicide bomber. Forty Americans were killed in Pennsylvania at 9:37 a. m., time of impact at this quiet, tranquil, country-side.

On September 11, 2001, terrorist intended to change America and they did. "Now flags are flying everywhere, families are brought closer together and new determination, even as they wiped away the tears." But, even as I write, war clouds continue to loom around us, making George Washington's hope of "Nation not rising against Nation" – as yet to become a reality.

After the attack, Americans prayed in groups and in solitude.

Central Virginians gather to pray, help

Pennsylvania crash

A Boeing 757 en route from
Newark, N.J., to San Francisco
crashed Tuesday near
Shanksville, Pa.

Bush: 'Freedom will be defended'

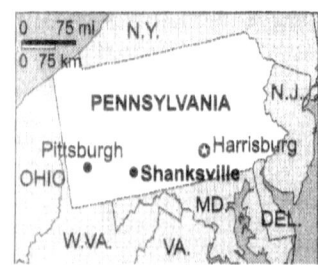

Copied from Lynchburg *News & Advance*

STEPPING BACK IN TIME:

Even in our old age, I still enjoy R. E. Marstin and his wife, Rhoda, and their stories from yesteryears! While visiting me recently, Rhoda told of her grandfather, Mr. Charlie Rush, of Red House, making coffins in his wood-working shop for the surrounding area. Some had a different reason for using them, they would salt down their pork meat in them in order to keep burglars out. Protection enough, I would say!

School teachers back in our school days were privileged to whip children and they did! R. E. told this one: For some reason, Miss Lucy Steptoe, their teacher at Hat Creek school, didn't have time to whip Charlie Marston on the day of his crime, but said "I will whip you tomorrow", Knowing that Miss Steptoe never broke a promise, Charlie's immediate attention turned to man's first law of nature, that of self-preservation. The next morning Charlie tied strings around the bottom of his pant's legs and stuffed them full of oak leaves. R.E. said the first stroke of Miss Steptoe's whip on Charlie's legs, broke the strings and the leaves came tumbling down and Miss Lucy Steptoe did keep her promise!!

Another of R. E.'s jokes was about a man who broke his leg back in the depression days. Someone asked, "How did you break your leg?" He said, "While I was eating breakfast this morning", "How was that?" he was asked, – "I fell out of the "simmon tree" During those days another man, R. E. said, went into a country store to buy a pair of overalls, even though the man being very short of statue, told the merchant that he wanted the longest pair he had. The merchant asked why he wanted such long ones, he said "I want to use the cut-off pieces for patches."

The ole country boys were recipients of many jokes back then, like this one who went to the city to buy his wife a girdle. The clerk, wanting to know something about the size asked, "What bust?" He said, "nothing bust, it just plain wore out."

Another ole country boy went to the city, so the story goes, and sorghum molasses, which was a regular on country tables was also being served on the city relative's table.

When asked if he would have some Molasses answered, "I ain't had none yet". Lasses had been good enough for him!

R. E's wit and humor came from his dad, our uncle Elva Marstin, who always kept us laughing at his stories. I never read the Biblical scripture about the rewards of being kind to your enemies, and by so doing, "Heaping coals of fire on his head", (Proverbs 25:22) that I am not reminded of one of Uncle Elva's favorite tales. It seems this old woman was complaining to her preacher about how cruel her husband was to her, the preacher asked her "Have you tried being kind to him, thereby heaping coals of fire on his head?" She answered, "No, but I've tried hot water."

Uncle Elva told of during World War I his Staff Sargent had them line up, each soldier holding out his right leg. The Sargent would eye the line from front to back, making sure they were all together. One soldier down the line was holding out his left leg. The Sargent yelled out "What fool back there is holding out both legs?"

One Sunday, Uncle Elva, Frances, Margaret and R. E. were at our house for lunch. Mama must have run short of vegetables for the stew that day, or as the need demanded, maybe, she thinned it more than usual. R.E. looked into his bowl and asked, "What did Aunt Mary do, drop a tomato in the well?" Recently when I reminded him of it, he said ,--"food was never short on Aunt Mary's table", and he was right.

THE LOVE OF MY LIFE:

Daddy having grown up in the Hat Creek Presbyterian Church, returned there on every possible occasion to worship with his brothers, Elva, Orin and sisters, Cornelia Elder and Nannie Bentley and their families. All devout Presbyterians, not only Presbyterians but HAT CREEK PRESBYTERIANS!! That was also enjoyment for us to visit there and to go with them home for lunch. One Sunday, while walking through the church yard with my cousins, Margaret and Frances, they paused to speak to a boy, Eldridge Carwile, who was sitting in his family car. As they passed a few words, I thought – never had I seen such bright blue eyes! Also on Saturday afternoon at times, daddy would take us to Hat Creek ball games, in which Eldridge was a star player. I enjoyed watching him pitch and joined in the cheering squad, as he pitched a no-hitter or would hit a home run. After the game he always "just happened" to come my way – but just casual friends.

CLASS OF 1937: (Front row, left to right) Ruby C. Harms, Bernice M. Gunther, Kathleen P. Gilliam, Ruth M. Carwile, Lois S. Groves; (2nd row) Mary D. Campbell, Rachel M. Paulette, Mary E. Parsons; (3rd row) Russell Carson, Larry Harper, Robert Carson.

Madisonville High School Reunion

When I graduated from Madisonville High School, I dared to send Eldridge an announcement. That night as I was leaving my group of classmates, he was waiting for me in the crowd, asking to take me home. Of course, I accepted and he also had for me a box of embroidered handkerchiefs, which he brought as a graduation gift (His grandmother had shopped for him.) Our class flower was the white rose of which Mrs. Gay Chambers had brought me a beautiful bouquet of them. Even now the memory of their sweet fragrance and the aesthetic joy merging on that special night still linger when I catch the aroma of the old fashion white rose – Oh the eternal gift and memory of true love that never grows old!!

Even though we did not date regularly we remained good friends. Once while Eldridge and his family were living in an old cabin on the farm, before building a short distance away, Mrs. Carwile gave Eldridge a birthday party. She sent a family member down for me and, of course, I went. Eldridge had been dating another girl and she was there with him as his honored guest. Needless to say, that was not the most enjoyable party I ever attended!! But, if only I could have had a crystal ball that night.... and could have foreseen that Eldridge and I would marry, spend ten years in that same house and that our son, Donald Eldridge, would be born while we were living there.

Looking much further into the future that our son, Dr. Don and his wife Dee would some day own that same house and farm. The Carwile farm since 1936 – now, at 83 years of age, I am still blessed with the privilege to maintain my home on this ancestral Carwile farm and to have my family near. Sometimes it seems, they say, "God writes straight with crooked lines" and I do thank Him for directing our paths thus far.

Eldridge went to work as a carpenter on the Pentagon building, which was under construction already – work having begun on the building in September, 1941 (completed in 16 months , by January 1943) Later, Eldridge came home to farm with his daddy who was in failing health and we were soon married, refurbishing the old house they had moved from. I loved the old cabin, a honeymoon cottage it could have been called. We painted the rooms, bought a new bedroom suit and some second-hand furniture, because of the war, new furniture was hardly available. We bought a table and chairs and a wood -burning cook stove for the kitchen. How happy we were even though there was very little money. Eldridge and I worked hard on the farm with his parents, growing tobacco for a meager income, but still with plenty of food. We canned from the summer gardens, raised chickens, hogs and had a milk cow. Having lived through the great depression, we thought we were well off - and were appreciative for what we had. I saved chicken feed bags for homemade dresses, sheets and pillowcases and made quilts from the scraps. Women in the community would exchange bags in order to have enough matching for a dress or some other needed project.

Carpenters at Pentagon Building

I bought a Singer treadle sewing machine which I have used all through the years, and still do, making most of my clothes, even suits and coats. My machine was one of the last steel heads to be made, an antique dealer recently told me that my sewing machine is the best kept one he has seen for its age. I took in sewing, carried eggs and butter to the store for necessary groceries and kerosene for the oil lamps. We bought an oil burning Aladdin lamp, which had a net-like wick, giving a white flame, a much brighter glow than the old oil lamps, but with one disadvantage, the wick was very fragile, and soon had to be replaced.

We drew water from a well in the yard, heated wash water on the kitchen stove and scrubbed clothes on a wash board -hanging them to dry on a line in the backyard. Flat irons were heated on the wood stove summer and winter. I used the back of Eldridge's worn out jeans to make front legs for others.

Mrs. Carwile
(Ruth's Mother-in-law)

Mr. Carwile
(Ruth's Father-in-law)

Ruth's Current Home

We had a battery powered radio and enjoyed entertainment, especially music from Nashville on Saturday nights. Also, Lum and Abner; Amos and Andy, Lone Ranger and others. Finally, electricity became available in our area, around 1948, we bought an electric radio, a black and white television, only available then. Ours being the first in the community, we had a house full of company every night. Our Lynchburg T .V. station just celebrated its 50th anniversary-started 1953.

"Sometimes it seems one can point to the time when a major shift in culture or history takes place. The year, 1948, is an example. When the year began there were 19 television stations broadcasting in the United States and Americans owned 186,000 TV sets. By the years end the number of television stations had doubled and 1,000,000 T.V. sets had been sold. We had entered the video age and nothing could turn back the clock. Few people could have guessed the amazing changes, both good and bad that would take place in American culture because of T.V." –copied

We bought an electric refrigerator and later a food freezer. Mr. Tom Joy added an electric motor and cord to my old push lawn mower. What an improvement!!

One day about dusk I went into the hen house to get eggs from the nest. I thought I was taking a half broken egg shell out of the nest to throw away – a black snake had the other half of the egg in its mouth. I soon agreed for him to have it!! My father-in-law, Tom Willie Carwile, came to my rescue and shot the snake.

Another day, I went in the hen house and a black snake was in the nest, I called on Eldridge's grandmother, Mrs. Lizzie Tucker, who was always willing to help me, she poured a kettle of boiling water on it – we were the ones that went scampering out!!

140

THE BIRTH OF OUR SON!!

On March 5, 1949, our son, Donald Eldridge Carwile was born in the old Lynchburg General hospital. After my winter days of sewing for him, his layette was ready. How happy we were and how delighted I was that he had his daddy's bright blue eyes!! Don was privileged from early childhood to grow up surrounded by loving and caring grandparents, Bernice and Tom Willie Carwile; also, great grandmother, Mrs. Lizzie Tucker, whom the grandchildren affectionately called "Ma Ma", and a great aunt, Miss Loza Elliott, whom they called "O", all of whom adored him. When he was a young child at times I would miss him from the yard and he would be going down the road to granny's house. I would call out "Don, where are you going"? His answer, "to the White house", their house being painted white, versus our unpainted one. Granny's house was a big attraction, besides, all those who would pamper him. He would get to play with his cousins, Scottie, Cheryl, Reecia Lou, and later Kathy, Merle's and Lois' daughters - also, Dorothy and Carroll's sons, Tilson and Jason.

When Don started to Brookneal Elementary School, I had realized early on that he would have no trouble learning. He had known exactly where the "The Golden Books" stands were located in every store –straight to them he would go, never tiring of having me read to him. His first grade teacher was Mrs. Hilda Tonkins, later Mrs. Sadie Marshall, Mrs. Ethyl Clowdis, and Mrs. Virginia Elder (now his mother-in-law) All dedicated teachers.

The same fall that Don started to school, we started building a new brick house further up the road, where I am privileged to still live. Eldridge, a skilled carpenter himself, working with Waverly (Kate) Harper, a renowned carpenter of the community worked all winter on our house. After waiting to grow another crop of tobacco, they resumed work on our house again in the fall. We never borrowed any money, we moved into our new home the following spring, March 1956.

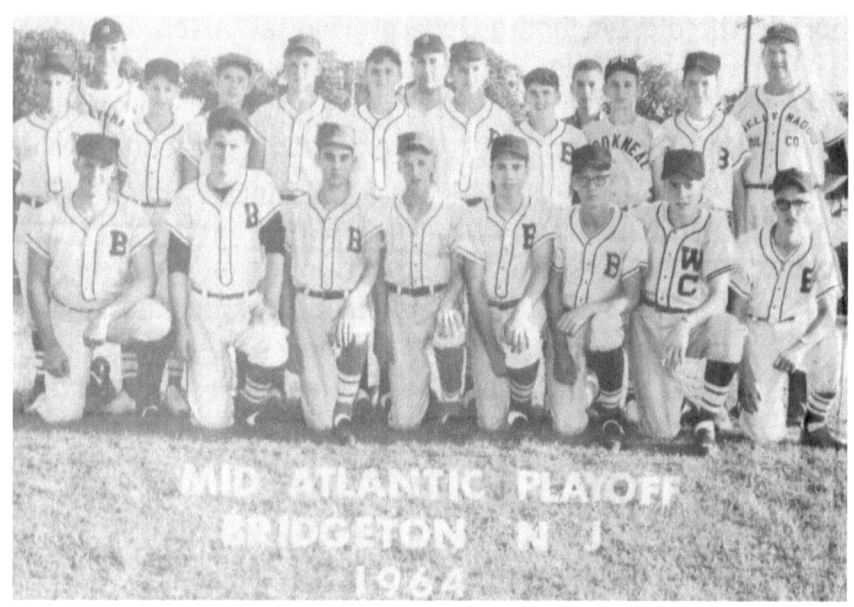

1964 Virginia State Babe Ruth Champions
20 years later, still winners!!!

We stayed busy here on the farm. All working together, with me juggling my time between church, school, room mother, shuttling Don and neighborhood boys to their ball games, and our community Home Demonstration club - there was never time for work outside of the home for me. In Don's growing up he and Eldridge were more like brothers in relationship than just father and son - working, hunting, and fishing together, along with Bob Foster and his sons, Jerry and David. Eldridge taught Don the things that enabled him to strike a happy medium between work-studies - and play. His dad taught him how to hold a bat and how to pitch a curve ball; also, once in a lifetime feat, in 1964, their "Babe Ruth team won state championship at Fort Belvoir, finally losing to New York in Bridgeton, New Jersey:

Dennis Elder, a star player, told this story: "After a four hour bus ride, we arrived at Fort Belvoir, ready to settle into the army barracks that would be our home for the next few days. We all got off the bus and stretched and looked around at the numerous identical barracks and dirt and gravel roads weaving in between them. Just then, a rabbit ran out from under one of the barracks and stopped in the middle of the road about a hundred feet away. The bus driver tapped me on the shoulder and said, ' let's see how good your arm is, hit that rabbit' I picked up a good sailing rock and proceeded to hit the rabbit in the back of the head. The bus driver stared in shock and then broke out into a deep laugh. "I'm putting the bus away and then I'm calling my wife and tell her that I won't be home anytime soon," he said, "After what I just saw, I know you guys are going to win the State Championship so we'll be here quite a while!

Eldridge also taught Don how to pitch a horseshoe, and even the exact angle to shoot a marble. Don still enjoys the great out doors here on the farm. During the summer months and on many weekends, during school year, my sister

Rachel Rice's son, Barry Rice, who lived in Lynchburg, spent those childhood times here on the farm with us. Just 15 days difference in age, Barry and Don grew up like brothers, working, playing together, playing string music, pitching horse shoes, hunting and fishing along with Eldridge.

Looking back over those years, I, like everyone else, will remember what I was doing another day that will go down in infamy, the day President John F. Kennedy was assassinated. Eldridge and I were in the attic of our house laying insulation, not hearing any news reports all day. We didn't know of it until Don came in from school that afternoon. The following Sunday we came in from church, turned on the TV and saw the live happening of his assassin, Lee Harvey Oswald, being shot by an assailant Jack Ruby as Oswald was being led into a room by officials – almost too much to conceive of in such a short period of time, totally unbelievable!!

Our home is located in a quiet, mostly law abiding section of Campbell County; a sheriffs' patrol car has always been an unusual sight on our county road. On this particular day, just before Christmas in the 60's I got up early, about light, eager to get my holiday chores done. Our pack of beagle hounds was barking in the yard, seemingly trying to devour something, which I thought was a stray dog. We never bothered to remove keys from the car ignition out on the yard or lock the car or even to lock our house; we felt so secure. Eldridge needed to go to the doctor in Brookneal that morning, while we were there Dr. Tune casually said, "Two desperados have escaped from a New Jersey prison, killing the guard, taking his gun and are believed to be headed this way." I did not connect his story about the escapees and the vicious barking of our dogs that morning. As we approached home that day, police cars were all around, searching all buildings on the farm, even searching the basement of our house. Board and Ella Dews, our neighbors, had seen two men walking down the road to our house that morning and then in a few minutes saw them go back up the road, thinking maybe, Eldridge was hiring some farm help for that day. When they saw them come down and then wondered why they suddenly came back up the road, they too, thought no more about it at the time. (I think Board always regretted the opportunity to have been the "crime stopper" of the day!!) Evidentially they crossed over through the woods to highway 615, now Red House Road, and because of the extreme cold, December temperature, they were forced to surrender to authorities the next day. They had made a fire near our house in the woods. The next summer as a neighbor, Tilden Foster, was cleaning out his hay barn, just up the road from my house where they had apparently slept, he found the gun which they had taken after killing the New Jersey prison guard. With the correct serial numbers, authorities were able to identify it as the "smoking gun" – I shall always be grateful that our beagles were on the alert that morning, no doubt saving us from becoming added victims of those desperados.

Beagle dogs have always been a part of our family life; I still think they are the most intelligent and affectionate of all dogs. Such a good mother, was one, Tootsie, after she had given birth to so many litters of pups herself, she seemingly thought all pups belonged to her. Another mother beagle had given birth to pups, Tootsie took over like they were hers. Still fulfilling her motherly instinct, she started nursing them, actually producing milk. I called Dr. Andrea Redd, of Halifax County Veterinarian Center, to confirm this and she said it is called "false pregnancy." – to Tootsie, it was nothing false about it.

Don, on completion of seventh grade, at Brookneal Elementary School graduated as valedictorian of his class. How proud we were as he delivered his well-prepared speech, which later, I carefully and prayerfully tucked away so that, if possible, he could some day use excerpts from it again in a High School valedictory speech. When Don started to William Campbell High School, in the eighth grade, each student was to meet with Mrs. Myrtle Staw, the guidance counselor, along with the mother, to schedule subjects in conjunction with the student's choices of vocation. I was a few minutes late in arriving for our appointment, Mrs. Straw said, "Come on in Mrs. Carwile, Don and I have already started, he says he wants to become a medical doctor and we are scheduling related subjects for him". After five years at William Campbell, lettering in sports, Beta Club President, SCA President, and many other activities, and yes... excerpts from his valedictory speech from Elementary School graduation were used as he so eloquently delivered it that night at his William Campbell High School graduation exercises!! (He was one of two valedictorians for his class.)

Don and Dee (his high school sweetheart)
as king and queen of their senior prom

Tops Three Ways

By Gene Hansley of Lynchburg News

William Campbell High School senior Don Carwile thinks his high achievement in one area of school life helps him reach top levels in other areas too.

Don is president of the school's Student Government Association, ranks second, academically, in a class of 90, and is in the starting lineup of the school's varsity football team.

"To be a good athlete," he said, "you have to put out and give it all you have, and being a good student is the same way."

He believes being a good student and playing on an athletic team plus participating in other school activities "go hand in hand."

Don was elected Student Government president last spring and now gives two or three hours a week to the job. But he says a lot of other people "help me right much" with the office.

He is studying English, government, physics, advanced math and Spanish for the second year. Don says he "usually studies" three hours a night, and with football practice every afternoon, he doesn't get home until 6:30 p.m. either.

When he studies, Don says he tries "to cover the most important things first, or anything I'm having trouble with."

His easiest subject "would be Spanish, but I like physics best. It's harder, but more interesting."

Interestingly enough, he does not think good grades are of first importance. "You should work to increase your knowledge. If you do, the grades will come."

Right now, he's beginning to think about the upcoming college board examinations, but he hasn't decided definitely which college he wants to attend. When he does go to college, it will be to prepare for a career in medicine.

"I've just always thought I'd like to work with and help people," he says.

In athletics, Don plays football and baseball. He is both safety and halfback and "I've quarterbacked some too," he said. He has scored seven points this year on a team which has won six games and lost only one.

He holds down center field on the baseball team. If forced to make a choice, Don says he likes both sports, "but I guess I'd have to say I like football better."

Besides all these activities, he belongs to the Beta Club, Monogram Club, Spanish Club, and Science Club.

Don is a quiet, soft-spoken young man with blue eyes, a rather solemn expression, and a modesty about his achievements.

He thinks there are "a lot of people who do well" academically while being active in athletics and many other school activities too.

Also he is part of that rapidly expanding group of students in high schools who respect more the student who does well in many areas than the ones who just achieve athletically.

William Campbell High School Student Government President Don Carwile

William Campbell High School Student Government President Don Carwile Oct. 1966

He Ranks Second, Academically, In Class of 90. Don Also Is
in Football Team's Starting Lineup.
(Later valedictorian)

Don's Valedictorian Speech, William Campbell High School

Don's Graduation, Hampden Sydney College

Dee as Valedictorian of her class
William Campbell High School

Local musicians enjoy playing for churches, special occasions

Five local musicians get together very once in a while and practice eir music, usually a few days fore they are to perform for a ocial event. The musicians are erman Ginther, guitar; Frazier emore, piano; Don Carwile, itar; Barry Rice, saxophone; and ean Jarvis, bass guitar.

Ginther told how the band got arted. "Frazier and I played gether in a dance band for a mber of years. Frazier and Barry t together at high school," he said. inther has been playing the clarinet for about 65 years.

Ginther said that when he, Rice, and Sizemore went to a local church to play not long after their band was formed a few years ago, they heard someone say they sounded "sick." So the band went out and recruited a doctor - Don Carwile.

Then, as Ginther's story goes, it wasn't long before someone in the audience said they needed to improve the looks of the band, so they got a younger man - Dean Jarvis.

Carwile said that Barry called him last summer and asked him to join the band. "I've been playing for about 20 years, I enjoy the fellowship of the guys. We get together and

practice and generally have a good time. Most people seem to enjoy it," explained Carwile.

The band has played for Brookneal Baptist Church, Falling River Baptist Church, Beulah Baptist Church, Ebenezer Church, Brookneal Presbyterian Church, Brookneal Methodist Church, Phenix Presbyterian Church, Mt. Terrah Baptist Church, Childrey Baptist Church, Forest Methodist Church, and Hat Creek Club House.

They play instrumental hymns, usually the old standbys, such as "Amazing Grace" and "The Old Rugged Cross." Dean Jarvis, who became involved with the band last

fall, said, "I would describe it as a cross between Dixieland jazz and gospel, just because of the instruments involved."

"I've really enjoyed playing with them," said Jarvis. "We get a lot out of it. We get a good feeling from making other people happy when they hear us."

Besides the enjoyment of playing with the band, Jarvis said he has learned a lot about music from the other members of the band. Jarvis plays the bass guitar, which he has been playing for about nine years.

Frazier Sizemore thoroughly enjoys his association with the no-name band. "It's an outlet. I like music - all kinds of music. It seems to be a natural thing to do, plus it keeps us out of devilment."

Sizemore described the group's style as "very informal. Each time we practice we try to add something new. For the hours we practice ... it takes your mind totally away from the trials and tribulations of the world."

Rice and Carwile, who are first cousins, have been playing music together since they were about 12 years old. Carwile's father, Eldridge Carwile who is now deceased, taught Carwile to play the guitar, and Rice would come down from Lynchburg to help on the farm, bringing along his saxophone.

"I played in some bands in high school and college and didn't play for about 20 years," said Rice.

When Rice was teaching a William Campbell High School a few years ago, he worked on a talent show where he played music with Jarvis and Frazier. Two years ago Debra Guthrie, who remembered that show, asked Rice to do a solo a Brookneal Baptist Church.

Rice asked Ginther and Frazier to assist him, and from that performance they were discovered. Someone from Ebenezer Baptist Church was in the audience and asked them to play for their church. Word-of-mouth advertising has kept

Please see Page 2

MUSICIANS – Local musicians, from left, Don Carwile, Dean Jarvis, Barry Rice, Herman Ginther and Frazier Sizemore, front, get together a couple of times a month to play gospel music for churches of all denominations in the area.

In the fall of 1967, Don entered Hampden-Sydney College, launching out in a pre-medical career. Working in the library most weekends for extra funds, when he would get paid, he would call Eldridge and me down to take us to Cedarbrook Restaurant in Farmville. He still wants to share.

After Don was established in Hampden Sydney and Eldridge doing carpentry work with my brother, Benny Marston, during the winter months, I decided to go to Ralph's School of Cosmetology in Lynchburg, some 35 miles away. After having been in training at Ralph's about seven months, on May 11, 1969, I received a telephone call that that Mr. Carwile, my father-in-law had been killed in a farm tractor accident. Devastated, I stayed home and helped on the farm that summer, returning to school in the fall. I was 50-years old, when I went to Richmond for my state boards; I received my Cosmetology license a few days later July 7, 1970, Eldridge and Benny built a shop in my back yard for me and I have had a steady flow of clientele, which I still maintain to a degree, even at age 83. Through my shop I have made many life-long friends.

After graduating from Hampden-Sydney College, Cum Laude, Don married his high school sweetheart, Mary Dee Elder from Brookneal. Dee by then had finished Longwood College. They moved to Richmond in the fall, Don in Medical School and Dee in Pharmacy at the Medical College of Virginia. Later, Don and Dee moved to Blackstone where he took his Family Practice training. After years there, where would he go from there?? Back home to Brookneal, of course!! For years he has been "Dr. Don" to so many. I remember when he was a child, my mother gave him a "doctor's kit" as a Christmas gift. He wore it out (and me , too) taking my temperature, and checking my pulse, and now how grateful I am that he is here and can check me for real!! Also, how thankful I am to have Don, Dee and family near by. Will, a graduate of Longwood College, is married to Lorie O'Brien; Sara Ellen, a graduate of Meredith College, is married to Brian Bowles; and Mary Anna, in William Campbell High School. My only regret is that Eldridge did not live to enjoy them more, and to see and know precious, Mary Anna. Eldridge did enjoy Will and Sara Ellen for awhile. Will enjoyed riding the tractor with him, sitting on Eldridge's lap, with Eldridge allowing him to "drive" the tractor. How Eldridge would have enjoyed his jovial personality now!!!

From: Centra Health's magazine, "A Gift to the Community"

Physicians

(Continued from page 4)

patient in the ambulance and they are on their way."

Nygaard said the patient's personal physician is a key in deciding treatment. "They know their patients very well, and often they pick up on subtle things that we might overlook. They are very important to us."

A Brookneal area native, Carwile has known since he was 10 that he wanted to be a doctor — a physician like his family doctor, Dr. William Cassada, who practiced in Brookneal for many years. "I always had the utmost respect and admiration for him. I wanted to follow in his footsteps."

An only child, Carwile grew up on his parent's flue-cured tobacco farm — a place where his mother and grandmother still live. He graduated from William Campbell High School, where he played football and baseball, and enrolled in Hampden-Sydney College. He chose the Medical College of Virginia for medical school, and completed his residency training at the Blackstone Family Practice Residency.

Carwile opened his Brookneal Family Practice Center in 1978 just months after finishing his residency. He knew he wanted to return home.

Carwile's office is prepared to handle a wide range of medical problems, from routine checkups to emergencies. "We are the closest thing to an emergency department for 30 miles both sides of Brookneal," he said. "We have to be prepared."

Carwile has no doubt he chose the right profession. "It gets close to me when people I have known all my life have bad diseases," he said, "but it is very rewarding when things go well."

Dr. Donald Carwile and Catherine Rosser

Personal Physicians Key In Care

Catherine Rosser had no warning. She felt fine as she chatted with customers in her job as teller at the Bank of Charlotte County in Brookneal. Then suddenly, she turned pale and fainted.

When rescue workers brought her to Dr. Donald Carwile's family practice office, she was ghostly white and had fainted a second time. Her electrocardiogram was abnormal. Diagnosing her heart problem, Carwile rushed her on to the Lynchburg General Hospital emergency department.

Before returning home, Catherine Rosser would need a cardiac catheterization and double bypass and valve surgery. That was in April. Today, she's back working at the bank and feeling great.

"I had a wonderful doctor," Rosser said. "That's the reason I came out of it at 78 years old, and it is just wonderful to be up and going about my work."

Carwile and his partner Dr. William Jones often refer pa-

tients to Lynchburg for cardiac catheterizations and surgeries. "We see a lot of heart problems in family practice," said Carwile.

Carwile and Jones kept track of Rosser while she was in Lynchburg. "The cardiologists are very good about giving us follow up information on patients while they are in the hospital and after discharge," said Carwile. "I've been super pleased. We have a good relationship and that's important for the welfare of the patient."

That strong relationship is also important to the cardiologists and cardiac surgeons. "We have a good relationship with our referring physicians," said Dr. Thomas Nygaard, Lynchburg cardiologist and director of the cardiac catheterization laboratories. "We want to serve as a referral center to provide the services they need, when they need them — anytime day or night. Some physicians may call us with a question. Others may call to say they've put a

(Please see page 20)

Don and Katherine Rosser

Sara Ellen, as a small girl, with an order pad and pencil, would go to Eldridge's chair, pretending to take his food order as a little waitress. He would name everything in the book as she would "write" them down, how precious are memories of those short-lived days – and how Eldridge would have loved Mary Anna with her angelic disposition. Especially this story: As a small girl, Mary Anna was to spend the night with me, Don and Dee were going out with another couple; when they brought her by she overheard Don tell me that if she decided to go home, he would come for her - that he had to do. A few days later I was baby sitting her, holding her closely in my lap, I asked her why she didn't want to spend that night with me, she said, "I had the arthritis". I do thank the Lord that I have been privileged to enjoy our precious grandchildren.

Will Carwile Sarah Ellen Carwile

Mary Anna Carwile

All was going well until on March 14, 1982, Eldridge had a fatal heart attack, devastating us, literally turning my world upside down. I shall always be grateful to my family, friends and shop clientele for bearing with me through those crucial days; I stayed busy and with the Lord's help, somehow I endured.

Rev. F. Marion Dick , a former pastor then living in North Carolina, wrote me many tines that the Lord was preparing me for widowhood in my cosmetology training and work, and now that I too, can plainly see.

Mary Frances Marston, daughter of Edna and E. O. (Life) Marston, an invalid from birth requested that I come to her home for an interview, wanting a slot in my book in praise and adoration for her cousins, Ryland Marston of Crewe, Benny, Renneth, and Kenneth Marston of Red House, Va. who recently purchased and delivered a motorized wheelchair to her home in Newport News (which she is pictured in).

Mary Frances is now living back in Lynchburg, Virginia running around at will in her apartment, out on her sunny deck, and even down a ramp onto her street!!! She is so happy with her new chair and with the mobility it affords, the first ever for her (Mary Frances is now 74 years of age.).

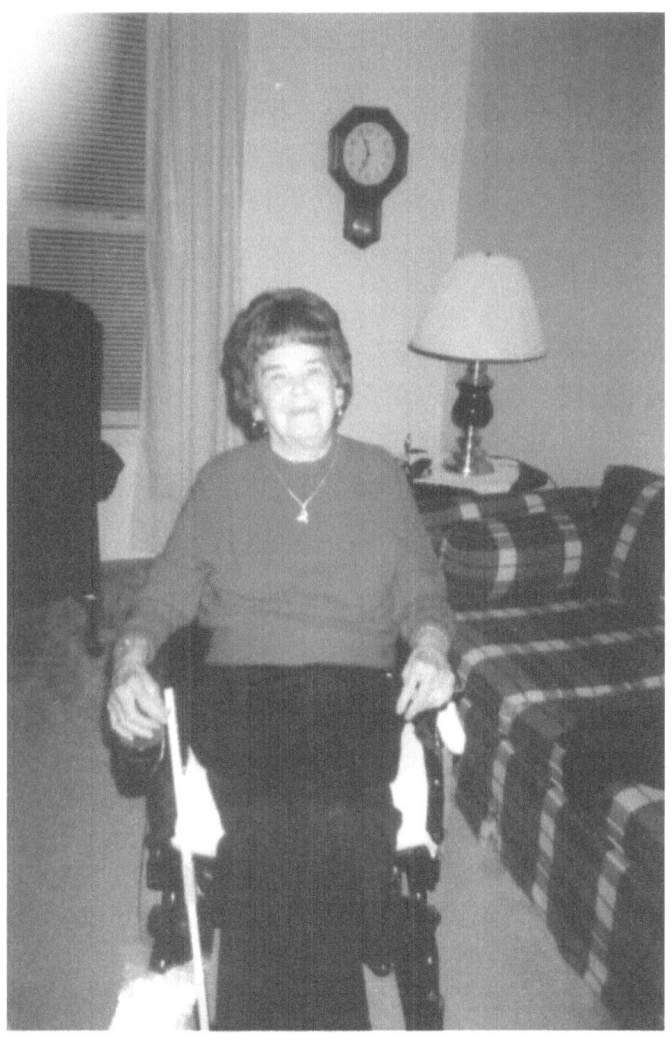

Mary Frances Marston

After her extensive expressions of love and thanks for her cousins, the Marston brothers, who donated it, I asked her for words that I might use. She said it all, "The chair is wonderful and they are too!!"

Knowing the low profile which Ryland, Benny, Renneth, and Kenneth maintain of their wide-spread acts of generosity, I hesitated to include this segment in my book without their consent, but with Mary Frances' persistence, I agreed. I, Ruth, could also fill an entire book on their many acts of kindness and support for me over the past years!!

MY DIVINE REVELATION

I am over 82 years old - no such experience before – It all began as a normal Sunday in October, 2001, nothing unusual about the church service, Leonard Oliver teaching a good Sunday School lesson, as usual, and Rev. John Jackson, our minister, delivering a good message and the children presenting a gift of song, I don't even remember the lyrics.

On the way home from church, driving down the highway, my mind reflected back to a scene from childhood, of us when we were small children, standing in front of the old Providence Church congregation singing, "Jesus Loves Me" – as I sometimes do while driving alone, (I'm not a singer) I started singing it. As I was finishing the first verse, I became aware of others singing with me....what could this mean? I stopped singing, and the beautiful voices and music continued on with the next verse: "Jesus Loves me / loves me still / though I'm very weak and ill / from His shining throne on high / comes to watch me where I lie / Yes, Jesus loves me / Yes, Jesus loves me / Yes, Jesus loves me / for the Bible tells me so" with the singing and music gradually moving out into the distance. I hesitate to tell this, but it was so real, I felt compelled to tell it, I didn't have the radio on. I don't feel deserving of such a revelation, but I do accept His grace and that is sufficient unto me!!!

IN CONCLUSION

I have tried to reveal to you, my readers, the qualities that make for a happy heart. They are not derived from materialism but, I believe, from courage, faith, humor - from the simple things of life. "There is something about simplicity that reconnects one with the earth in this world of high speed and technology. It not only reconnects one with the earth, but with God...O, to see the Creator God in simplicity today"!!

Someone asked Billy Graham, now in his old age; also, what advice he would like to give to young people. His answer, "I would like to remind them of the brevity of life." Also, I would like to reinforce his words with truths from the 90th Psalm. "For a thousand years in thy sight are but yesterday when it is past, and as a watch in the night.

"Thou carriest them away as with a flood; they are as asleep: in the morning they are like grass which groweth. In the morning it flourisheth, and groweth up; in the evening it is cut down, and withereth. We spend our years as a tale that is told. The days of our years are threescore years and ten; if by reason of strength they be fourscore years, yet is their strength labor and sorrow; for it is soon cut off, and we fly away. So teach us to number our days, that we may apply our heart unto wisdom." -KJV

As you my readers have journeyed with me from the "horse and buggy" days to the computer age I am reminded of a skeptic, Henry Eldsworth, who like me "In My Wildest Dreams" could never have conceived of the changes which have taken place since my childhood continuing through my 83-years. I read that Henry Eldsworth, a member of the U.S. Patent Office said, "It might as well be closed there is nothing left to invent." He said this before the McCormick reaper and Morse telegraph had been thought of. I too, thought we were as modern as could ever be, especially as a mode of travel - our beautiful green 1928 Chevrolet car! Yet, it was beyond "My Wildest Dreams" when on July, 20, 1969 a space ship carrying three astronauts: Neal Armstrong, Mike Collins and Buzzy Alden landed on the moon. How thrilling to watch TV from our living rooms as they planted our beloved US Flag, Old Glory, on this celestial body revolving around the earth!! Neal Armstrong called it "One small step for man and one giant step for mankind."

Also, on a Christmas Eve, 1972, Astronauts sent pictures back from the moon of this planet of ours, so brilliant, so beautiful, a globe of green and blue in a midnight sky. How moving as one astronaut read from Genesis I...God's wonders never cease!!

GROWING OLD?

They say that I am growing old!
I have heard them tell it times untold
In language plain and bold –
But I am not growing old
This frail old shell in which I dwell
Is growing old, I know full well,
But I am not the shell!

What if my hair is turning gray!
Gray hairs are honorable, they say.
What if my eyesight's growing dim –

I can still see to follow Him
Who sacrificed His life for me
Upon the cross of Calvary.
What should I care if time's old plough
Has left its furrows on my brow?
Another house not made with hands
Awaits me in the Glory Land.
What though my tongue refuse to talk…
I can still tread the narrow way.
I can still watch and praise and pray.
My hearing may not be as keen
As in the past it may have been
Still I can hear my Saviour say
In whispers soft, "This is the way."
The outward man, do what I can
To lengthen our life's short span.
Shall perish and return to dust
As everything in nature must.
The inward man, the Scriptures say,
Is growing stronger every day.
So how can I be growing old
When safe within my Saviour's fold?
'Ere long my soul shall fly away
And leave this tenement of clay-
This robe of flesh I'll drop and rise
To seize the everlasting prize.
I'll meet you on the streets of gold
And prove that I'm not growing old!

-Author unknown

SEIZE THE MOMENT . . . SEIZE THE DAY!!!

MY THANKS to all who have contributed stories, pictures, and support in compiling and writing my book; especially to my sister, Charlotte Arrington for her many endeavors in typing my book. Also, my sincere acknowledgment to the many historians who have edited facts and figures, which I used from various sources in my memoirs. To the best of my knowledge and belief, all historical material used is factual and available to the public domain.

Ruth M. Carwile

About the Author

Today, November, 1999, as I, Ruth Marston Carwile, stand on the brink of another year, another century and yes, another millennium and also my eightieth birthday, I will try to portray to you, my readers, some of the changes which I have witnessed over the span of those years:

I, like every young person, hoped and dreamed of a prosperous fulfilling life, but in my wildest dreams and youthful imagery could never have foreseen the dramatic changes in scientific and medical technology, social and economic development and in every phase of life, as I have seen transpire over the past 50 years. I once had a Sunday School teacher who, in her mind, would explain in metaphor, how all inventions, discoveries, etc. are made possible for us. She said they are as apples already on a tree which God lowers, within reach of man, giving him the ability to attain them, and the natural gifts and talents to develop them, in His own Providential time and way.

If that be true, never before in history has God been so busy "lowering apples" nor has He given mankind so much knowledge, skill and ability to develop them as in the past 50 years. Even today, when we are so blessed as never before with modern conveniences, technology, etc., each new day brings newness on the horizon, with much of the old becoming obsolete. After so many changes, the carnal mind tells me that there cannot be many more "apples" left on the tree to be developed, but the Spiritual instincts ring out loud and clear - "My Father worketh still and so do I" John 5:17!! Please follow me now as I reflect on these ever changing times.